Cashing in on the Consulting Boom

Gregory F. Kishel
Patricia Gunter Kishel

A Wiley Press Book

JOHN WILEY & SONS, INC.

New York ● Chichester ● Brisbane ● Toronto ● Singapore

Publisher: Stephen Kippur
Editor: Theron Shreve
Managing Editor: Katherine Schowalter
Composition & Make-up: Ganis & Harris, Inc.

Library of Congress Cataloging-in-Publication Data

Kishel, Gregory F.
  Cashing in on the consulting boom.

  Includes index.
  1. Business consultants. I. Kishel,
Patricia Gunter. II. Title.
HD69.C6K53   1985   658.4'6   85-12376
ISBN 0-471-81695-7

Printed in the United States of America

85 86 10 9 8 7 6 5 4 3 2 1

Contents

Preface

The most important product any consultant has to sell is his or her ideas and information, skills and abilities. In effect, as an independent consultant, you will be paid for your knowledge, for what you can do and can convey to others. Among those who have embarked on successful consulting careers are: students right out of school, managers and technicians who want to establish their own businesses, retirees eager to put their years of experience to profitable use, college professors, and teachers. Whatever your area of expertise, be it engineering or employee relations, physical fitness or product design, there's likely to be a demand for your consulting services.

By definition a consultant is someone who works independently, providing the specialized services and advice that organizations and individuals need to achieve their goals. Such occupations as sales trainer, health care specialist, electronics expert, investment counselor, and entertainment planner illustrate the diversity within the consulting industry. More often than not consultants are asked to assume the role of problem-solver, helping clients to make decisions, meet deadlines, and raise performance levels. Depending on the nature of an assignment, you may meet the client one time only or you may develop a professional relationship spanning several years. As for your fees, these can be set in a variety of ways ranging from an hourly rate to a monthly retainer agreement.

Cashing In on the Consulting Boom provides a complete plan for converting your knowledge and experience into a successful consulting practice. As active consultants ourselves, we have designed this book to take the mystique out of being a consultant. Step-by-step, it examines all aspects of becoming an independent consultant, from choosing your field and setting up the business to determining fees, meeting with clients, and marketing your services. Whether your consulting practice is still in the idea stage or is already established, you'll find here the information you need to make it grow.

1

Who Needs Consultants?

A MORE direct question than "Who needs consultants?" would be "Who *doesn't* need consultants?" Consulting-industry revenues are increasing at an annual rate of approximately 20 percent. What was a $32 billion industry in 1980 has more than doubled since then. The field of management consulting alone accounts for over $4 billion in annual revenues and keeps more than sixty thousand consultants employed on a full-time basis. Given the rising demand for consulting services, it appears that virtually everyone needs the help of one kind of consultant or another. Government agencies, businesses, and nonprofit organizations are turning to outside consultants with increasing frequency both to keep fixed costs down and to obtain the most up-to-date information. At the same time, individuals now seek the advice of consultants on personal and professional matters ranging from planning finances to choosing a wardrobe; from charting a career to hosting a dinner party.

WHY CLIENTS HIRE CONSULTANTS

There are many reasons behind the current consulting boom. Chief among them is the complexity of our day-to-day lives. Regardless of their capabilities, organizations and individuals are finding it difficult, or impossible, to accomplish their goals single-handedly. For example, if a business wants to expand its advertising coverage, it has thousands of media from which to choose, including over seventy thousand different newspapers and magazines and more than ten thousand radio and television stations. As individuals become more health-conscious and concerned about the artificial additives in their foods, it takes more than a passing knowledge of the seven basic food groups to plan their diets. To make the right decisions, complete tasks properly, use resources efficiently, and take advantage of existing opportunities, expert advice or assistance is often needed.

Situations That Require Consultants

Each of the following situations would commonly require the services of a consultant, and each represents a type of problem that consultants are frequently called upon to solve.

The Client Has a Deadline to Meet

One of the main reasons for hiring a consultant is that the client simply can't finish what needs to be done in the time available for its completion. A business that needs to line up additional distributors in time for a key buying season is an example of this situation. A government agency that has to gather specific research information prior to an upcoming Senate hearing is another. So is the individual who must have his or her tax return ready to file on April 15. In these situations, the client needs someone who can start work immediately and has the ability to achieve the desired outcome.

The Client Lacks the Expertise to Do the Job

Often a consultant is called in when the client is faced with a situation that requires specialized skills, training, or knowledge. Few organizations and individuals possess the necessary qualifications to make all the decisions or perform all the tasks that require their attention. Utilizing consultants is a way to obtain the expertise they need. For example, an organization that wants to install a more efficient phone system would be likely to engage the services of a telecommunications consultant. An individual who has reached a career impasse might seek out a career-development consultant for help in deciding what action to take.

The Client Has a Personnel Shortage

Consultants can be a cost-effective means of combating temporary personnel shortages. Rather than having to go through a lengthy process to find, recruit, hire, and train a new employee, the client can avoid this by using a consultant. Speeding up the selection process in this way saves the client not only time but also money. Even when the consultant's fee is higher than an employee's salary would be, there still can be a significant saving. This is because the consultant is not eligible to receive the benefits (vacation, holiday and sick pay, insurance, pension, and other compensation) that employees receive in addition to their salaries. These benefits typically amount to over 35 percent of a worker's annual salary.

The Client Needs an Objective Viewpoint

A good consultant brings more than expertise to an assignment; he or she brings an objective viewpoint. Whereas the client or the client's staff may be used to seeing the situation in a certain way, the consultant sees it without preconceived ideas. This objectivity can be invaluable, enabling the consultant to come up with innovative solutions to problems and to make unbiased recommendations. Unlike employees, who are often afraid of losing their jobs or of alienating their co-workers, consultants have no such fears. Because the consultant doesn't stand to win or lose on the basis of the changes that are implemented, the client feels confident of getting an honest opinion.

The Client Wants to Capitalize on the Consultant's Credibility

When a recommendation or assessment comes from an outside consultant, it generally has more credibility than it would coming from an employee, relative, or friend. The higher the consultant's level of expertise and objectivity, the higher the credibility. Having a certified public accountant examine a corporation's accounting records each year not only meets a legal requirement but also reassures shareholders that the organization is being truthful with them. Hiring a real estate appraiser to determine the current market value of a home serves a similar purpose, in this case verifying what the property is really worth.

The Client Wants to Avoid Going through Channels

Utilizing the services of a consultant is often desirable when a client wants to get quick results or protect confidential information. Rather than going through normal channels, which might be more time-consuming and involve more people, the client brings in a consultant to do the job. For example, a business that wants to win government contracts might hire a government marketing consultant with contacts in Washington, D.C. The consultant would be in a better position to find out about contract opportunities than someone who is unfamiliar with the way the government operates. Other types of consultants that businesses use when they want to avoid going through channels include consultants in such fields as investigations, security systems, new-product development, marketing research, new ventures, and banking.

The Client Wants to Avoid a Conflict

In order to avoid conflicts within their own businesses, it's not uncommon for clients to hire consultants to carry out controversial or politically charged assignments. Overseeing a company's reorganization plan, negotiating the terms of a union contract, rating a department's efficiency level, choosing between one strategy and another are all examples of this. By having a consultant make the decision or perform the task, the client is able to disassociate himself or herself from the proceedings. Thus, any ill feelings that result will be directed toward the consultant rather than the client.

Later, once the consultant has left, it will be easier for all parties involved to resume their normal working relationships.

The Client Is Experiencing a Crisis

Not surprisingly, clients also expect consultants to bail them out of trouble when a crisis hits. Consultants might be used when: a client is facing bankruptcy; consumer groups are complaining; quality control levels have dropped; additional capital is needed; a lawsuit has been filed against the client; the client's health is endangered; an important decision must be made. Whatever the nature of the crisis, the client needs someone to step in and turn the situation around, successfully dealing with the problem and saving the day.

The Client Wants a Second Opinion

In many instances, the reason for hiring a consultant is simply to prove (or disprove) the client's previous findings. The need for a second opinion isn't just confined to the medical field; having the benefit of an additional viewpoint can be advantageous in a number of fields. Consultants frequently asked to provide second opinions include medical and legal consultants, engineering experts, management consultants, marketing researchers, tax advisers, and public opinion pollsters.

The Client Doesn't Wish to Perform the Task

In some instances, even though the client could perform the task, he or she prefers not to do it. Perhaps it isn't cost-effective for the client to perform the task or the client finds the task distasteful. Other possibilities include: the client wants the status that comes from utilizing a professional to carry out the assignment; the client has a budget surplus and must "use it or lose it." Under these circumstances, using a consultant allows the client to accomplish the task while satisfying a personal need as well.

SERVICES CONSULTANTS PROVIDE

The types of services that consultants provide run the gamut from furnishing clients with information and advice to actually supervising or performing the work that needs to be done. Following are some of the more common services that consultants provide.

Researching

Consultants often help clients by gathering information and conducting in-depth studies, such as researching the impact of proposed legislation or consumers' reactions to a new product. Depending on the scope of the research assignment, this can involve obtaining *secondary data* or *primary data*. Secondary data is information that is already in print or readily available from recognized sources. Primary data is information based on first-hand observations, surveys, or experiments.

Advising

The service for which consultants are best known is advising—making recommendations on the specific courses of action that clients should follow. Recognizing the value of expert advice, many businesses have gone so far as to establish permanent advisory boards to aid their top managers and corporate directors. Individuals also have been quick to utilize consultants, asking them for advice on how to advance their careers, improve their financial standings, and enjoy life more.

Planning

One of the consulting services that has been in great demand in recent years is planning, more specifically the area of "strategic planning." In an effort to meet competitive challenges and keep pace with rapidly changing technologies, businesses are intent on devising strategies, or overall plans, for reaching their objectives. Some consulting firms have become so adept at helping clients to set objectives and develop the policies and procedures for attaining them that they no longer offer any other types of services.

Evaluating

Sometimes what the client really wants is for the consultant to rate the effectiveness of an existing method or approach to a problem. A consultant might be asked to evaluate, among other things, a client's current advertising campaign, inventory control system, employee compensation plan, office layout, or physical-fitness program.

Training

As jobs become more specialized and employees must continually upgrade their skills, the need for consultants' training services increases constantly. Consultants are meeting this need by developing specialized training programs that can enable employees to improve their technical, human-relations, and administrative skills. Utilizing personal instruction, films, videocassettes, workbooks, and computer simulations, consultants are helping employees to be more productive in their current jobs and preparing them for advanced positions.

Supervising

In addition to advising clients on the best ways to achieve their goals, many consultants also assume the role of supervisor, making sure that their recommendations are carried out correctly. This can entail supervising the client's staff, the consultant's own staff, or independent contractors. Types of consultants who would normally provide clients with supervision services include architectural and engineering consultants, interior designers, caterers, and conference planners.

CONSULTING TRENDS

What does the future hold for the consulting industry? Which types of consulting services will be in demand? How will consultants fare in comparison to others in the labor force? The answers to these questions and more will depend largely on the changes that occur in our society's economy, our political environment, new technology, and our lifestyles in general.

The Economy

The consulting industry, as a whole, is one of the few industries that is virtually unaffected by economic cycles. When the economy is strong, consultants do well since clients can easily afford to hire them. When the economy is weak, consultants still do well since clients become more dependent on them for their services. Within the consulting industry itself, though, the demand for particular consulting services can fluctuate. For example, during periods of high employment, the demand for specialists in employee selection, training, and relocation should rise as businesses compete with each other for the most qualified workers. Conversely, the demand for career-development consultants would be likely to drop, due to the widespread availability of jobs.

The Political Environment

The power of our political institutions to enact legislation, tighten or loosen regulations, and increase or decrease government spending can have a profound effect on the demand for consultants. Whenever there is a change in the laws, this creates a demand for consultants who can interpret the change and advise clients on how to comply with the new law. Stricter antipollution regulations will result in a greater demand for pollution control consultants; weaker regulations will cause the demand to diminish. Budget cutbacks in one area can force those agencies that have been affected to hire fewer consultants. On the other hand, agencies whose budgets have been expanded will be able to hire more consultants.

Technology

The development of new technologies creates a demand for consultants who are familiar with the technologies and can assist clients in implementing them. Computers, electronics, communications, medicine, engineering, manufacturing, and agriculture are just a few of the fields that are undergoing large-scale technological changes. Even the arts aren't immune to the impact of modern technology, as evidenced by the growing interest in computer-generated graphics and holograms (three-dimensional pictures produced by reflected laser light).

Lifestyles

Individual lifestyles must also be taken into consideration. As the number of working women and two-paycheck families continues to grow, so does the demand for consulting services. Instead of taking the time to gather information themselves or perform various tasks, individuals are relying more heavily on consultants. Some of the consultants who have benefited from this lifestyle change include wardrobe planners, color consultants, interior designers, party-entertainment specialists, financial planners, and investment counselors. Our society's increasing health-consciousness has also created opportunities for consultants, especially those in the nutrition and physical-fitness fields.

In addition to monitoring these areas to detect consulting trends, it's important to keep a close watch on your competitors. Who are they? What types of services do they offer? What are their fees? How do they solicit consulting business? Keeping track of the competition will provide you with a better understanding of your industry and help you to identify new consulting trends.

2

Picking Your Field

MOST consultants discover early in their careers that it's not possible to be all things to all people. Attempting to be the jack-of-all-trades of consulting is to invite disaster. For one thing, knowledge that is highly valued in one industry may be of little importance in a different industry. Ironic as it seems, the very qualities that enable you to excel in a particular area can hold you back in another. To achieve success as a consultant, you must define what it is you have to offer and how your experience can best be applied. What you are able to accomplish, how others see you, and how you see yourself hinges, in part, on picking the consulting field that is right for you.

Perhaps you have already identified the consulting field you would like to enter. Or you may be investigating several alternatives. In either case, how can you be certain of making the best choice? Will the type of consulting practice you elect to start provide the financial and emotional rewards you are seeking? Even though, of course, there are no sure things in business, you *can* increase the probability of your success by taking certain factors into consideration. These factors include the economy, political environment, technology, client needs and preferences, and the competition. The single most important factor of all, though, is you. Just because a consulting business is right for a friend or colleague doesn't mean it is right for you. Nor is specializing in the "hot" consulting topic of the moment necessarily the answer. To be the "right" choice, the consulting field(s) you pick must truly reflect your interests and qualifications.

INTERESTS

In weighing the pros and cons of the various consulting fields from which to choose, start by asking yourself, "What really interests me?" For now anyway, set aside the issues of qualifications and the needs of the marketplace and examine your own needs. Selecting a consulting field that matches your interests is crucial, because you're not just investing a sum of money or even time in a business; you're investing part of yourself. It's vital that you enjoy what you do and feel challenged and excited by the consulting assignments you are asked to perform. This is the number one prerequisite for attaining professional satisfaction and giving clients the quality of service they deserve.

The list that follows should help you to get in tune with your own interests. Rather than being an exhaustive catalog of every interest imaginable, this list is intended to stimulate your thinking. Once you've thought about which of these interests—and any others you want to add—relate to you, write them down on a separate sheet of paper. The more interests that can be incorporated into your consulting activities, the better. For instance, if you are interested in working with people in groups, enjoy problem-solving, researching, and training, you should pick a consulting field that will allow you to pursue these interests. Three possible such fields are employee selection and training, career guidance, and small-business development.

TYPES OF INTERESTS

Working independently	Working with numbers and statistics
Working with people in groups	Working with computers

Working with machines	Designing
Working with your hands	Drawing or painting
Working outdoors	Writing
Working indoors	Speaking
Researching	Training
Analyzing	Traveling
Managing	Enhancing people's personal
Organizing	appearance
Problem-Solving	Enhancing people's health
Investing	Enhancing people's quality
Creating or inventing	of life

QUALIFICATIONS

Listing your interests was the first step toward picking a consulting field. The next step is to take a personal inventory of your qualifications—the experience, educational background, and skills that you have to draw upon. By examining your strengths and weaknesses in each of these areas, you can gain a clearer idea of the various fields for which you are currently suited.

Experience

Experience is the best teacher. To determine what you can do as a consultant, start by looking at what you have already done in the past. Write down the jobs you have held, the tasks you have performed, and the activities in which you have taken part. In going over your experience, don't limit yourself to just paid work experience. Be sure to include volunteer and life experience as well. If you served on a fund-raising committee for a charitable organization, include that. Or, if you were a military "brat" as a child and have lived in several foreign countries, that should be included, too.

The goal here isn't just to write out a list of job titles. It's to get at the essence of what each job entailed and the experience you gained in carrying it out. It's also to increase your awareness of the experience you have acquired that's unrelated to work. For instance, suppose you had worked in advertising, volunteered to help in a political campaign, and were an amateur photographer. The experience you gained from these activities might include the following:

TYPES OF EXPERIENCE

Work	*Experience Gained*
Advertising researcher	Helped to develop advertising campaigns; used organizational and time-management skills to complete projects and meet deadlines; worked with copywriters, art directors, and clients; conducted focus group interviews to obtain customer information; compiled and used demographic data.
Nonwork	
Political campaign volunteer	Canvassed neighborhoods; operated phone bank; helped organize mailings; accomplished tasks on short notice.
Amateur photographer	Learned to use a light meter and various lenses and filters; know how to develop and print black and white pictures.

After you've completed this section of your personal inventory, examine it closely to identify any trends or consistencies in the types of experience you have had. Two such consistencies stand out in the example just given. Conducting focus group interviews is a similar experience to canvassing neighborhoods, since both involve questioning people to obtain their opinions. Meeting deadlines and accomplishing tasks on short notice also match each other. While you are spotting these consistencies, you should also make note of which types of experience you enjoyed the most and which types you disliked.

Educational Background

In going over your educational background, apply the same method you used to inventory your experience. It's important to write out more than the usual two-line listings of schools attended and degrees received. Write down the subject areas you have studied and the specific classes you have taken. You should include any seminars or workshops you have attended for the purpose of maintaining or improving your skills or to familiarize yourself with a new field.

In our own case, for example, we both have Master of Business Administration degrees. When the various courses we've taken are compared side by side, however, it becomes apparent that our educational backgrounds are not identical. In addition to the standard management curriculum, Gregory took specialized courses in labor arbitration, transportation systems, and investments and securities. Patricia's studies, on the other hand, included classes in consumer behavior and advertising strategies. Thus, while we both hold the same degree, each of us has a different reservoir of knowledge. This knowledge is available to us to use in our consulting practice if we so choose, just as the academic knowledge you have gained can be used in your practice. Naturally, what gets used and what doesn't depends on which consulting field you pick.

Skills

Your experience and educational background make up two-thirds of your qualifications. The remaining third is comprised of your skills—the specific abilities that you can bring to bear in performing your consulting activities. Those skills most frequently cited as being necessary for success as a consultant can be broken down into five types: technical

know-how, communication skills, familiarity with human
relations, administrative skills, and self-motivation.

Technical Skills

Technical skills are the abilities that enable you to provide
your consulting services—the ability to design buildings, sell
products, manage money, coordinate wardrobes, train employees, research new markets, increase efficiency, solve
problems, and so on. A consultant who knows about the laws
and tariffs that apply in importing and exporting goods has
technical skills. So does a consultant who is able to design,
conduct, and interpret opinion polls. Other types of technical skills include teaching, engineering, writing, computing,
operating equipment, programming, cooking, drawing,
practicing medicine, organizing, and accounting. Of course,
the list doesn't stop here. There are as many types of
technical skills as there are types of knowledge and abilities.

Communication Skills

Communication skills are what enable you to express yourself and to understand others so that ideas and information
can be shared. Making a phone call, preparing a report,
giving a presentation, reading a trade journal, writing a
letter, and meeting with a client all require communication
skills. The various communication skills used by consultants
include speaking, writing, reading, and listening. Combined,
they often take up the majority of a consultant's day. Depending on the type of consulting you do, some skills may be
used more than others. The one used by all consultants, and
generally regarded as the most important, is listening. Only
by listening can you determine the full extent of your clients'
needs and concerns and whether or not they are pleased
with your services.

Human-Relations Skills

Human-relations skills can best be defined as the ability to
get along with others; to inspire confidence, cooperation,

and loyalty. Consultants sometimes make the mistake of thinking that the only thing that counts is their ability to carry out an assignment—their technical skills. Nothing could be further from the truth. The relationship between a consultant and a client is a fragile one, based on trust and the attainment of mutual goals. To maintain it—and the repeat business and client referrals that go with it—you must be able to establish a rapport with the people you meet. This entails empathizing with their feelings, adjusting to their habits and preferences, and exhibiting a caring attitude.

Administrative Skills

Administrative skills are what keep a consulting practice going. The more adept you are at managing your resources of time, money, people, and property, the more profitable your consulting practice will be. Consultants with poor administrative skills are at a distinct disadvantage when it comes to keeping track of the everyday details of running a business. Although they may be good at performing individual assignments, they overlook or ignore such equally important activities as setting goals, marketing their services, and collecting fees. For your consulting practice to progress beyond the start-up stage and develop into a viable business, administrative skills are a necessity.

Self-Motivation Skills

Self-motivation skills are what keep *you* going. Successful consultants are self-starters. They possess the drive (both mental and physical) to accomplish the tasks of their choosing. Rather than waiting for something to happen or expecting someone to tell them what to do, they create their own opportunities. What's more, they derive much of their satisfaction from their work itself, viewing it as a rewarding activity, rather than as just a means to an end. The major difference between self-motivated people and others is their ability to maintain their enthusiasm and to set new challenges for themselves.

SPECIALIST VERSUS GENERALIST

In picking the consulting field that appeals to you the most, you must also decide whether you want to be a *specialist* or a *generalist*. Consultants who are specialists make it a point to know as much as possible about a particular subject or industry, such as electronic security systems or the banking industry, and limit their work to whatever area they choose. Consultants who are generalists prefer to look at the big picture, cultivating knowledge that can be applied in several areas, rather than just one. Management consultants, who provide a variety of services to different types of clients, would fit into this latter category.

The thing to remember in choosing between becoming a specialist and becoming a generalist is not to define your services too narrowly or too broadly. If you define your services too narrowly, you run the risk of excluding prospective clients who might be able to benefit from your knowledge. On the other hand, if you define your services too broadly, your credibility as an expert will be diminished.

In addition to considering the scope of your knowledge and services, you should also give some thought to which aspect of problem-solving you prefer—the diagnosis or the implementation. In other words, would you rather identify a problem or solve it? Generalists, as a rule, spend more time diagnosing problems. Specialists, who usually aren't brought in until after a problem is known, spend more time actually implementing the necessary changes.

TYPES OF CONSULTING FIELDS

The list that follows should help to illustrate the many different types of consulting fields that one can enter. Whether your interests and qualifications are in computers or community relations, interior design or inventory control, new ventures or nutrition, there is likely to be a consulting field that matches them. Far from being complete, this list is just the beginning. As technologies, work situations, lifestyles, and the environment continue to change, additional demands will arise for the advice and information that consultants can provide.

TYPES OF CONSULTING FIELDS

Accounting
Acoustics
Advertising
Agriculture
Aircraft and Aerospace
Apparel and Textiles
Appraisal
Architecture
Assertiveness Training

Banking
Budgeting
Building Management
Business
Business Communications

Career Development
Catering
Chemistry
Civil Engineering
Color
Communications
Community Relations
Computers
Conference Planning
Construction
Contest Planning
Conventions
Credit and Collection

Data Processing
Direct Mail
Drug and Alcohol Abuse

Education
Electrical Engineering

Electronics
Employee Compensation
   and Benefits
Employee Relations
Employee Relocations
Employee Selection and
   Training
Employee Surveys
Employment Services
Energy
Engineering
Entertainment

Fiber Optics
Financial Planning
Food Services
Foreign Licensing
Franchising
Fund Raising

Geriatrics
Government Marketing
Government Regulations
Government Relations
Graphic Design

Health Care
Heating and Air
   Conditioning
Hospitalization Insurance
Hotel Management

Import-Export
Industrial Operations
In-House Publications
Insurance

Interior Design
Inventory Control
Investigation Services
Investment Counseling

Labor Relations
Landscaping
Law
Leasing
Lie-Detector Testing
Lighting
Lithography

Management
Manufacturing
Marketing
Marketing Research
Materials Management
Medicine
Merchandising
Mergers and Acquisitions
Minorities

New-Product Development
New Ventures
Nutrition

Office Design and Layout
Organization Behavior
Organization Development

Packaging
Personnel
Physical Fitness
Plant Design and Layout
Plant Security
Plastics
Politics
Pollution Control
Pricing
Printing
Product Design

Production Management
Public-Opinion Polls
Public Relations
Publishing
Purchasing

Quality Control

Real Estate
Recreation
Research and Development
Retailing
Risk Management

Safety Engineering
Sales Forecasting
Sales Management
Sales Promotion
Sales Training
Salvage and Reclamation
Security Systems
Shipping and Receiving
Small Business Development
Strategic Planning

Tax Planning
Telecommunications
Testing
Time and Motion Study
Time Management
Training
Transportation

Urban Planning
Utilities Management

Video Recording

Wardrobe Planning
Warehousing
Wholesaling
Writing

3

Setting Up Your Business

POSSESSING the knowledge and expertise to be a consultant is one thing; establishing a practice and running it successfully can be something else. What's needed here aren't vast sums of investment capital or a client list a mile long, but something much more basic and essential—a business plan. Before you can help others to achieve their goals, you must first set goals of your own . . . then take the appropriate steps to meet them.

START WITH A PLAN

Having chosen the field(s) in which you want to consult, your first impulse may be to rush out and get business cards printed, pick up the phone and start calling prospective clients. Don't—not without developing a plan of action. Taking the time to answer some key questions in the beginning will save you time (and money) later. For instance, start by asking yourself:

- Is my consulting practice going to be a part-time or a full-time operation?
- Will clients come to my office or will I go to theirs?

- Do I want the business based in my home or an outside location?
- What furnishings or equipment do I need?
- What licenses or permits am I required to obtain?
- Which legal form is best for me—a sole proprietorship, partnership, or corporation?
- What kinds of insurance should I have?
- How much should I charge for my services?
- Which individuals or institutions are most likely to want what I have to offer?
- What image do I want to convey?
- How can I maintain good client relations?
- What revenues do I project for the year?

It's important to answer these questions and more at the outset. The resultant business plan you create will help you to direct and coordinate the various activities connected with your consulting practice. In addition to this, it gives you the edge when it comes to making the best use of your resources. Instead of going after any and all clients, you can focus on your best prospects. And once you've scheduled a meeting, there's a greater likelihood that an actual consulting assignment will follow.

Some of the issues we've raised, such as setting your fees, marketing your services, and meeting with clients, will be discussed in separate chapters later in the book. For the moment, though, let's start with the basics: selecting the location for your consulting practice; determining what supplies and equipment you will need; obtaining the necessary licenses, permits, and insurance; and choosing the legal form that is best for you. Once you've addressed these nuts-and-bolts aspects of starting a business, your consulting practice will be several steps closer to opening its doors.

YOUR LOCATION

The location you select for your consulting practice will play an important role in its development, influencing your methods of operation, ability to serve clients' needs, and ultimate earnings potential. You should therefore consider each of the following alternatives before deciding which type of office location will work best for you:

- Homebased office
- Convenience office
- Shared office
- Private office

Each has its own advantages and disadvantages, all of which you should bear in mind. Then, based on your budget, working habits, types of clients, and desired image, you can select the location that is most appropriate for your needs.

Homebased Office

Many beginning consultants—and established ones, too—choose to work out of their homes. One of the main advantages of this choice is the money you can save by not having to rent office space. Since rent payments are often the single largest expense in running a business, your savings here can be significant. In addition to lowering your overhead, locating your consulting practice at home makes you eligible for a number of tax deductions. Specifically, it allows you to deduct a part of the operating and depreciation expenses on your home. In other words, a percentage of your mortgage payments or rent, depreciation, property taxes, insurance, utilities, and expenses for household maintenance, repairs or improvements is deductible. Details on how and when to take advantage of these deductions are discussed in Chapter 12.

But running your consulting practice from your home has other advantages besides financial ones, including the personal freedom to work whenever you choose, rather than adhering to a nine-to-five schedule; increased family togetherness; reduced stress associated with trying to be two places at once (your home *and* your office).

On the minus side, however, bear in mind that a homebased office isn't for everyone. First of all, there's the matter of space. You will need to set aside, at the very least, space for a desk and chairs, filing cabinets, and any supplies or equipment used in your consulting practice. And if you're planning to hold meetings with clients at your office, working out of your home may be impractical, depending on the distance you are from your clients and the kind of image you want to project.

There's also your temperament to consider. Some consultants find that they accomplish more if they actually leave the house each day and go to an outside office at a separate location. Separating your work environment from your home environment in this way can stimulate a feeling of professionalism. And finally, you should consider that outside offices generally provide more privacy than homebased offices, thus keeping distractions to a minimum and perhaps making clients more relaxed.

Convenience Office

Faced with the choice of working at home or establishing an outside office, a growing number of independent consultants are discovering a middle ground—the convenience office. Sometimes called "executive office suites," these offices provide consultants and others with working space and a host of amenities that might otherwise be too costly for their budgets. Located in buildings designed especially for convenience offices, each office is a separate unit but has access to a central reception area, conference rooms, and support services such as telephone answering, typing, and photocopying. Some convenience office complexes even offer their tenants the use of telex and accounting services, video equipment, teleconferencing, and on-site travel ticketing. For the consultant who wants the benefits of a private office and a full staff—without the bother of full-time maintenance—this could be the answer.

Beware, however: convenience comes at a price. Although leasing a convenience office is generally less expensive than setting up an outside office complete with office equipment and full-time secretary, it still isn't cheap. And when you add up the total cost of the various services, you may find that you've exceeded your budget. In as much as these services are usually offered on an à la carte basis, it's easy to do. In evaluating convenience offices and determining which, if any, is right for you, make note of each facility's layout and appearance, tenant mix, types of services provided, costs, and administration.

To find out more about convenience offices, you might start by contacting two of the leading companies in this field:

H.Q. Services and Offices
3 Embarcadero
San Francisco, CA 94111

Omni Offices
577-E Peachtree Dunwoody Rd., NE
Atlanta, GA 30342

Each of these companies has convenience office leasing facilities throughout the United States and can provide you with information about what's available in your area.

Shared Office

A simple and effective solution to your office-space needs may be to team up with another consultant and share. Consultants whose practices complement each other—such as an architect and an interior designer, a physical-fitness adviser and a nutritionist, or a management consultant and a marketing specialist—often do this as a matter of course. Not only does a shared office help to keep overhead expenses down, but officemates often prove to be good sources of client referrals. And when one consultant is out of the office, having the other to cover the phones is a way to reduce the cost of support services.

In order for this alternative to work for you, it's essential to find an officemate with whom you are compatible, both professionally and personally. In addition to having similar space requirements for your respective consulting practices, you should agree on how much to spend on rent and furnishings, the kind of image that best suits you, and how clients are to be treated.

If an appropriate officemate doesn't come to mind or you're reluctant to enter into a lease agreement, maybe "desk space" in an existing office will fill the bill. In this instance, you would sublet space in another office that has the extra space available. For example, real estate appraisers frequently set up shop in real estate brokerage or savings and loan offices. The amount of space rented in this situation can range from a desk and chairs with a telephone to a separate office suite with full support services.

Private Office

Leasing and furnishing a private office involves a greater commitment of your resources than the other alternatives discussed, but it also gives you the most control over your environment. Without having to make compromises with family members, building administrators, or officemates, you can set up your consulting practice exactly the way you want it. To save the expense of a secretary, many consultants find that an answering service or automatic answering machine works fine for them. Typing and bookkeeping, particularly when you're just starting out, can probably be handled by a part-time employee or outside service.

If you're thinking of locating your consulting office in a newer building in the heart of the central business district, make sure that your projected revenues justify the expense. Is this, in fact, where your potential clients will be? Is it the best location from which to serve them? Would an office in an older, less expensive building meet your needs and theirs just as well? Would it matter if your office were located outside the central business district? The thing to avoid here is falling victim to the "mahogany-desk syndrome"—spending so much on office space and furnishings that the business itself is put in jeopardy.

SUPPLIES AND EQUIPMENT

Each type of consulting practice has its own unique requirements for supplies and equipment. For example, a career guidance consultant needs to maintain a reference library on the present and future state of the job market. Along with this, videotape equipment may also be required to make tape recordings of clients in simulated job interviews. A product designer, on the other hand, has different needs: a drafting table and drawing supplies, perhaps even a computer with graphic design capabilities.

While your consulting practice is still in the early stages, there's no need to purchase all your supplies and equipment at once. Instead, make a list of the absolute essentials you will need to perform your initial consulting assignments. These items—stationery, work materials, office equipment, furniture, and fixtures—should then be obtained as economically as possible. To get your money's worth, be sure to compare the pros and cons of leasing versus buying furnishings and equipment. Whenever feasible, try to buy used items. And, to save money on repairs later, read the fine print on warranties and maintenance agreements.

Obtaining the supplies and equipment you will use in your consulting practice doesn't have to be a costly and unnerving experience. By using some ingenuity, you can get the things you need and still stay within your budget. For instance, office furnishings and equipment (including computers) can often be bought at public auctions. Stationery and other supplies can be purchased at discount office supplies stores.

LICENSES, PERMITS, AND INSURANCE

To keep your consulting practice legal and to protect yourself against liabilities, it's important to obtain any licenses or permits that are required, along with adequate insurance coverage. What you need depends on the nature of your consulting practice and where it's located. The following information should help you to make the appropriate decisions in this area. As an added measure, you may also want to confer with an attorney or insurance agent.

Business Tax and Permit

In order to operate your consulting practice, it may be necessary for you to obtain a business tax and permit, commonly known as a *business license*. This is usually issued by the city and/or county in which a business is located and is valid for one to two years. The fee for it, which is based on your gross revenues, can range from less than $50 to more than $100. To find out if consulting practices located in your area are required to have a business license, contact the office of the City Clerk in your municipality.

Occupational License

To maintain set standards of performance and guard the safety of consumers, most states regulate entry into certain consulting fields, such as health services, engineering, and accounting. If you will be consulting in a regulated field, you must first meet the standards set forth by the state licensing board governing your occupation. Once you have demonstrated your competence, you will be issued a license. Most licenses are valid for a period of one to two years, at which time they are renewable. To determine if an occupational license is required for your consulting field, check with your state's Department of Consumer Affairs.

Fictitious Business Name Statement

If your consulting firm's name is different from your own name (e.g., Creative Consultants; The Nutrition Specialists), then you will probably have to file a fictitious business name statement with the county clerk's office. The purpose of this statement is to make available to the public your identity and the identities of any others who are co-owners in your consulting firm. As a rule of thumb, a fictitious name statement would be called for in the following situations:

- When the surnames of all owners are not included in the consulting firm's name.
- When the existence of additional owners is suggested by the consulting firm's name (e.g., Jones and Associates; The Abbott Consulting Group; Campbell and Company).
- When the name of the consulting firm (if it is a corporation) is not included in its articles of incorporation.

Consultants who are active in more than one field or who want to spin off separate businesses from their consulting practices can file more than one fictitious business name. In our own case, for instance, we have the following fictitious business names: K & K Enterprises, Kishel Consulting Group, The Business Builders, American Business Press, and The Entrepreneur's Newsletter.

The time to file a fictitious name statement is within forty days after your consulting practice commences operations. This process involves (1) filing the statement with the county clerk, and (2) having the statement published in a newspaper of general circulation. The second part is to ensure that the public has an opportunity to see your statement. To save time and simplify the process, instead of going to the county clerk's office first, go directly to the newspaper where your statement will appear. Most newspapers carry fictitious name forms as a convenience to their customers and will not only file the completed statement for you but will also assist you in filling it out. The total cost for filing and publishing the statement should be somewhere between $25 and $75.

A MAIL CERTIFIED COPIES TO:

NAME _____

ADDRESS _____

CITY _____

B PUBLISH IN NEWSPAPER:

COUNTY CLERK'S FILING STAMP

FICTITIOUS BUSINESS NAME STATEMENT

THE FOLLOWING PERSON(S) IS (ARE) DOING BUSINESS AS:

1: Fictitious Business Name (s)

2: Street Address, City & State of Principal place of Business   Zip Code

3.

Full Name of Registrant

Residence Address

City   State   Zip

(if corporation, show state of incorporation)

Full Name of Registrant

Residence Address

City   State   Zip

(if corporation, show state of incorporation)

Full Name of Registrant

Residence Address

City   State   Zip

(if corporation, show state of incorporation)

Full Name of Registrant

Residence Address

City   State   Zip

(if corporation, show state of incorporation)

4. This business is conducted by ( ) an individual,   ( ) individuals (Husband & Wife),   ( ) a general partnership,   ( ) a limited partnership
( ) an unincorporated association other than a partnership,   ( ) a corporation,   ( ) a business trust   (CHECK ONE ONLY)

5A.

Signed _____

Typed or Printed _____

5B. If Registrant a corporation sign below:

Corporation Name _____

Signature & Title _____

Type or Print Officer's Name & Title _____

This statement was filed with the County Clerk of _____ County on date indicated by file stamp above.

6. New Fictitious Business Name Statement

7. Refile — Statement expires December 31.

File No. _____

I HEREBY CERTIFY THAT THIS COPY IS A CORRECT COPY OF THE ORIGINAL STATEMENT ON FILE IN MY OFFICE.

_____
COUNTY CLERK

BY _____ DEPUTY

File No. _____

Employer Identification Number

If you employ one or more persons in your consulting practice, the federal government requires you to have an employer identification number. This enables the government to verify that you are paying all appropriate employer taxes and withholding the proper amounts from employee paychecks. Even if your consulting practice is a one-person operation without any employees, it's still advisable to obtain an identification number, primarily because clients often need it for their records. And if you should decide to hire someone later, take in a partner, or incorporate your business, you will need the number for tax purposes.

It's an easy matter to get an employer identification number for your consulting practice. What's more, there is no fee for it. To obtain one, all you need to do is fill out IRS form number SS-4 and submit it to the Internal Revenue Service.

Form **SS-4** (Rev. 8-76)
Department of the Treasury
Internal Revenue Service

Application for Employer Identification Number
(For use by employers and others as explained in the Instructions)

1 Name (True name as distinguished from trade name. If partnership, see Instructions on page 4)

2 Trade name, if any (Enter name under which business is operated, if different from item 1)

3 Social security number, if sole proprietor

4 Address of principal place of business (Number and street)

5 Ending month of accounting year

6 City and State

7 ZIP code

8 County of business location

9 Type of organization ☐ Individual ☐ Partnership ☐ Other (specify) ☐ Governmental ☐ Nonprofit organization (See Instr. on page 4) ☐ Corporation

10 Date you acquired or started this business (Mo., day, year)

11 Reason for applying ☐ Started new business ☐ Purchased going business ☐ Other (specify)

12 First date you paid or will pay wages for this business (Mo., day, year)

13 Nature of business (See Instructions on page 4)

14 Do you operate more than one place of business? ☐ Yes ☐ No

15 Peak number of employees expected in next 12 months (If none, enter "0") ▶ | Nonagricultural | Agricultural | Household

16 If nature of business is manufacturing, state principal product and raw material used

17 To whom do you sell most of your products or services? ☐ Business establishments ☐ General public ☐ Other (specify)

18 Have you ever applied for an identification number for this or any other business? ☐ Yes ☐ No
If "Yes," enter name and trade name (if any). Also enter the approximate date, city, and State where you first applied and previous number if known. ▶

Date | Signature and title

Telephone number

Please leave blank ▶ | Geo. | Ind. | Class | Size | Reas. for appl. | **Part I**

Seller's Permit

In obtaining the various licenses and permits you need to operate your consulting practice, you should also investigate the possibility of getting a seller's permit. If you plan to sell products in addition to providing consulting services, and your state is one of those that taxes retail sales, then a seller's permit will be necessary. For instance, consultants who market their information via audiocassettes, newsletters, and books are likely to need seller's permits. So are interior designers who sell furniture and accessories to their clients, and nutritionists who sell vitamins.

A seller's permit (1) exempts you from paying sales tax on the merchandise you purchase from suppliers to resell through your consulting firm, and (2) authorizes you to collect the sales tax from your clients/customers. In addition, a seller's permit enables you to gain entry to product trade shows and to purchase goods at wholesale prices.

Although there is no fee for a seller's permit, you may be required to post a bond, depending on your estimated gross sales of taxable merchandise. This bond is to ensure that you collect and remit to the state all sales tax due. To find out more about the seller's permit and if you need one, check with your state's tax board.

Trademark, Copyrights, and Patents

As an independent consultant, your main stock in trade is knowledge. To protect your ideas and inventions, you should be aware of the purposes and uses of trademarks, copyrights, and patents.

Trademarks

Consultants, perhaps even more than other entrepreneurs, depend on customer loyalty and referrals to generate sales. Creating a recognizable name for your consulting firm is one way to increase your visibility and build up your practice. Having created such a name, though, you want to make sure that you derive the full benefits from it. This can frequently be accomplished by registering the name as your business's trademark.

By definition, a trademark is any word, name, symbol, device, or combination of these used to identify the products or services of a business and to distinguish them from those of other enterprises. To qualify as a registerable trademark, your name or symbol must not be confusingly similar to any existing trademarks of consulting firms in your field. Ideally, it should have positive connotations, be distinctive and easy to pronounce. Note that you cannot trademark your surname as the name of your consulting firm or products since anyone else with the same last name would be free to use it too. However, if you create a distinctive logotype that incorporates your name or initials into the graphic design, *that* can be trademarked.

Once granted, a trademark is good for twenty years and may be renewed indefinitely. Although you are not legally required to register your trademark at all, in as much as this gives you the greatest protection, it is definitely advisable. You can find out more about how and when to use a trademark by writing to the U.S. Department of Commerce, Patent and Trademark Office, Washington, D.C. 20231. Ask them to send you their pamphlet "General Information Concerning Trademarks."

TRADEMARK APPLICATION, PRINCIPAL REGISTER, WITH DECLARATION (Individual)	MARK (identify the mark)
	CLASS NO. (if known)

TO THE COMMISSIONER OF PATENTS AND TRADEMARKS:

NAME OF APPLICANT, AND BUSINESS TRADE NAME, IF ANY

BUSINESS ADDRESS

RESIDENCE ADDRESS

CITIZENSHIP OF APPLICANT

The above identified applicant has adopted and is using the trademark shown in the accompanying drawing[1] for the following goods: _____

_____ ,

and requests that said mark be registered in the United States Patent and Trademark Office on the Principal Register established by the Act of July 5, 1946.

The trademark was first used on the goods[2] on _____ ; was first used on the goods[2] in
      (date)

_____ commerce[3] on _____ ;
    (type of commerce)   *(date)*

and is now in use in such commerce.

4

The mark is used by applying it to[5] _____

_____

and five specimens showing the mark as actually used are presented herewith.

6

_____ .
         (name of applicant)

being hereby warned that willful false statements and the like so made are punishable by fine or imprisonment, or both, under Section 1001 of Title 18 of the United States Code and that such willful false statements may jeopardize the validity of the application or any registration resulting therefrom, declares that he/she believes himself/herself to be the owner of the trademark sought to be registered; to the best of his/her knowledge and belief no other person, firm, corporation, or association has the right to use said mark in commerce, either in the identical form or in such near resemblance thereto as may be likely, when applied to the goods of such other person, to cause confusion, or to cause mistake, or to deceive; the facts set forth in this application are true; and all statements made of his/her own knowledge are true and all statements made on information and belief are believed to be true.

_____
        (signature of applicant)

_____
        (date)

Form PTO - 1476 **(Rev. 10-82)** *(Instructions on reverse side)*   Patent and Trademark Office - U.S. DEPT. of COMMERCE
          (over)

REPRESENTATION

If the applicant is not domiciled in the United States, a domestic representative must be designated. See Form 4.4.

If applicant wishes to furnish a power of attorney, see Form 4.2. An attorney at law is not required to furnish a power.

FOOTNOTES

1   If registration is sought for a word or numeral mark not depicted in any special form, the drawing may be the mark typed in capital letters on letter-size bond paper; otherwise, the drawing should be made with india ink on a good grade of bond paper or on bristol board.

2   If more than one item of goods in a class is set forth and the dates given for that class apply to only one of the items listed, insert the name of the item to which the dates apply.

3   Type of commerce should be specified as "interstate," "territorial," "foreign," or other type of commerce which may lawfully be regulated by Congress. Foreign applicants relying upon use must specify commerce which Congress may regulate, using wording such as commerce with the United States or commerce between the United States and a foreign country.

4   If the mark is other than a coined, arbitrary or fanciful mark, and the mark is believed to have acquired a secondary meaning, insert whichever of the following paragraphs is applicable:

a) The mark has become distinctive of applicant's goods as a result of substantially exclusive and continuous use in _____ commerce for the five years next preceding the date of filing
(type of commerce)
of this application.

b) The mark has become distinctive of applicant's goods as evidenced by the showing submitted separately.

5   Insert the manner or method of using the mark with the goods, i.e., "the goods," "the containers for the goods," "displays associated with the goods," "tags or labels affixed to the goods," or other method which may be in use.

6   The required fee of $175.00 for each class must be submitted. (An application to register the same mark for goods and/or services in more than one class may be filed; however, goods and/or services and dates of use, by class, must be set out separately, and specimens and a fee for each class are required.)

Form PTO - 1476 (Rev. 10 - 82)   Patent and Trademark Office · U.S. DEPT. of COMMERCE

Copyrights

In addition to safeguarding your name, you can also safeguard your creations. One of the tools that enables you to do this is the copyright. Although most commonly associated with literary works, copyright protection extends to graphic designs, paintings, sculpture, musical compositions, sound recordings, and audiovisual works. Given this broad coverage, many consultants can benefit from copyright protection. A sampling of works that come within the scope of copyright coverage includes: reports, charts, technical drawings, graphic designs, computer programs, advertising copy, photographs, catalogs, brochures, newsletters, books, audiocassettes, and video recordings.

Copyrighting any of your creations is relatively simple. All you need to do is provide public notice of the copyright on the work itself and file an application for copyright registration. The fee for this is $10, and you should be able to complete the paperwork by yourself. Once granted, a copyright is valid for up to fifty years after the holder's death. For more information on copyrights, write to the Copyright Office, Library of Congress, Washington, D.C. 20559. Make sure to specify the type of work you would like to copyright so that you receive the appropriate information and registration form.

FORM TX
UNITED STATES COPYRIGHT OFFICE

APPLICATION FOR COPYRIGHT REGISTRATION
for a
Nondramatic Literary Work

REGISTRATION NUMBER
TX   TXU
EFFECTIVE DATE OF REGISTRATION
Month   Day   Year

DO NOT WRITE ABOVE THIS LINE. IF YOU NEED MORE SPACE, USE CONTINUATION SHEET

---

①
Title

TITLE OF THIS WORK:

PREVIOUS OR ALTERNATIVE TITLES:

If a periodical or serial give: Vol ...... No...... Issue Date ....

PUBLICATION AS A CONTRIBUTION: (If this work was published as a contribution to a periodical, serial, or collection, give information about the collective work in which the contribution appeared.)
Title of Collective Work: .... Vol....... No ..... Date .... Pages..............

---

②
Author(s)

IMPORTANT: Under the law, the "author" of a "work made for hire" is generally the employer, not the employee (see instructions). If any part of this work was "made for hire" check "Yes" in the space provided, give the employer (or other person for whom the work was prepared) as "Author" of that part, and leave the space for dates blank.

1

NAME OF AUTHOR:

Was this author's contribution to the work a "work made for hire"?   Yes...... No......

AUTHOR'S NATIONALITY OR DOMICILE:
Citizen of .... } or { Domiciled in ....
(Name of Country)   (Name of Country)
AUTHOR OF: (Briefly describe nature of this author's contribution)

DATES OF BIRTH AND DEATH:
Born .... Died ....
(Year)   (Year)

WAS THIS AUTHOR'S CONTRIBUTION TO THE WORK:
Anonymous?   Yes...... No......
Pseudonymous? Yes...... No ......
If the answer to either of these questions is "Yes, see detailed instructions attached.

2

NAME OF AUTHOR:

Was this author's contribution to the work a "work made for hire"?   Yes...... No......

AUTHOR'S NATIONALITY OR DOMICILE:
Citizen of .... } or { Domiciled in ....
(Name of Country)   (Name of Country)
AUTHOR OF: (Briefly describe nature of this author's contribution)

DATES OF BIRTH AND DEATH:
Born .... Died ....
(Year)   (Year)

WAS THIS AUTHOR'S CONTRIBUTION TO THE WORK:
Anonymous?   Yes...... No......
Pseudonymous? Yes...... No......
If the answer to either of these questions is "Yes, see detailed instructions attached

3

NAME OF AUTHOR:

Was this author's contribution to the work a "work made for hire"?   Yes...... No......

AUTHOR'S NATIONALITY OR DOMICILE:
Citizen of .... } or { Domiciled in ....
(Name of Country)   (Name of Country)
AUTHOR OF: (Briefly describe nature of this author's contribution)

DATES OF BIRTH AND DEATH:
Born .... Died ....
(Year)   (Year)

WAS THIS AUTHOR'S CONTRIBUTION TO THE WORK:
Anonymous?   Yes...... No......
Pseudonymous? Yes...... No......
If the answer to either of these questions is "Yes, see detailed instructions attached.

---

③
Creation and Publication

YEAR IN WHICH CREATION OF THIS WORK WAS COMPLETED:

Year..........
(This information must be given in all cases.)

DATE AND NATION OF FIRST PUBLICATION:
Date................
(Month)   (Day)   (Year)
Nation................
(Name of Country)
(Complete this block ONLY if this work has been published.)

---

④
Claimant(s)

NAME(S) AND ADDRESS(ES) OF COPYRIGHT CLAIMANT(S):

TRANSFER: (If the copyright claimant(s) named here in space 4 are different from the author(s) named in space 2, give a brief statement of how the claimant(s) obtained ownership of the copyright.)

• Complete all applicable spaces (numbers 5-11) on the reverse side of this page
• Follow detailed instructions attached
• Sign the form at line 10

DO NOT WRITE HERE
Page 1 of .... pages

EXAMINED BY:	APPLICATION RECEIVED:	
CHECKED BY:		FOR COPYRIGHT OFFICE USE ONLY
CORRESPONDENCE: ☐ Yes	DEPOSIT RECEIVED:	
DEPOSIT ACCOUNT FUNDS USED: ☐ ·	REMITTANCE NUMBER AND DATE	

DO NOT WRITE ABOVE THIS LINE. IF YOU NEED ADDITIONAL SPACE, USE CONTINUATION SHEET (FORM TX/CON)

PREVIOUS REGISTRATION:

- Has registration for this work, or for an earlier version of this work, already been made in the Copyright Office?   Yes . . . . No . . . .
- If your answer is "Yes," why is another registration being sought? (Check appropriate box)
  - ☐ This is the first published edition of a work previously registered in unpublished form.
  - ☐ This is the first application submitted by this author as copyright claimant.
  - ☐ This is a changed version of the work, as shown by line 6 of this application.
- If your answer is "Yes," give: Previous Registration Number . . . . Year of Registration . . . .

⑤ Previous Registration

COMPILATION OR DERIVATIVE WORK: (See instructions)

PREEXISTING MATERIAL: (Identify any preexisting work or works that this work is based on or incorporates.)

{ . . . .

MATERIAL ADDED TO THIS WORK: (Give a brief, general statement of the material that has been added to this work and in which copyright is claimed.)

{ . . . .

⑥ Compilation or Derivative Work

MANUFACTURERS AND LOCATIONS: (If this is a published work consisting preponderantly of nondramatic literary material in English, the law may require that the copies be manufactured in the United States or Canada for full protection. If so, the names of the manufacturers who performed certain processes, and the places where these processes were performed *must* be given. See instructions for details.)

NAMES OF MANUFACTURERS	PLACES OF MANUFACTURE
. . . .	. . . .

⑦ Manufacturing

REPRODUCTION FOR USE OF BLIND OR PHYSICALLY-HANDICAPPED PERSONS: (See instructions)

- Signature of this form at space 10, and a check in one of the boxes here in space 8, constitutes a non-exclusive grant of permission to the Library of Congress to reproduce and distribute solely for the blind and physically handicapped and under the conditions and limitations prescribed by the regulations of the Copyright Office: (1) copies of the work identified in space 1 of this application in Braille (or similar tactile symbols); or (2) phonorecords embodying a fixation of a reading of that work; or (3) both.

  a ☐ Copies and phonorecords   b ☐ Copies Only   c ☐ Phonorecords Only

⑧ License For Handicapped

DEPOSIT ACCOUNT: (If the registration fee is to be charged to a Deposit Account established in the Copyright Office, give name and number of Account.)

Name: . . . .

Account Number: . . . .

CORRESPONDENCE: (Give name and address to which correspondence about this application should be sent.)

Name: . . . .

Address: . . . . (Apt.)

. . . .
(City)   (State)   (ZIP)

⑨ Fee and Correspondence

CERTIFICATION: ✱ I, the undersigned, hereby certify that I am the: (Check one)

☐ author ☐ other copyright claimant ☐ owner of exclusive right(s) ☐ authorized agent of: . . . .
(Name of author or other copyright claimant, or owner of exclusive right(s))

of the work identified in this application and that the statements made by me in this application are correct to the best of my knowledge.

Handwritten signature: (X) . . . .

Typed or printed name . . . . Date . . . .

⑩ Certification (Application must be signed)

MAIL CERTIFICATE TO

. . . .
(Name)

. . . .
(Number, Street and Apartment Number)

. . . .
(City)   (State)   (ZIP code)

(Certificate will be mailed in window envelope)

⑪ Address For Return of Certificate

✱ 17 U.S.C. § 506(e): Any person who knowingly makes a false representation of a material fact in the application for copyright registration provided for by section 409, or in any written statement filed in connection with the application, shall be fined not more than $2,500.

⚬ U. S. GOVERNMENT PRINTING OFFICE : 1977 O − 248−641

Patents

The other major tool that enables you to safeguard your creations is the patent. If, in the course of carrying out your consulting activities, you develop a product, process, or design that you believe has commercial possibilities, obtaining a patent may be advisable. In granting a patent to an inventor, the federal government gives him or her the right to exclude all others from making, using, or selling the patented invention in the United States. Design patents, covering only the style or appearance of a product, are granted for periods of three and one half, seven, or fourteen years, as specified in the patent application. Patents for new and useful products or processes are valid for seventeen years.

Obtaining a patent is considerably more involved than applying for a trademark or copyright. To do it properly, the federal government advises inventors to seek out the help of an attorney or agent skilled in preparing patent applications. The total cost, including the government's filing and issuing fees, is usually between $1,500 and $3,000. Given the potentially high stakes involved if your invention is indeed a winner, proceed with caution. It's important to be informed each step of the way throughout the patent-application process. To get the basic facts on obtaining a patent, write to the U.S. Department of Commerce, Patent and Trademark Office, Washington, D.C. 20231. Ask them to send you their pamphlet "Patents and Inventions: An Information Aid for Inventors."

Insurance

There is no point in setting up your consulting practice if you don't take adequate measures to protect it. In addition to protecting your ideas and inventions, it's important to protect yourself and your practice against financial losses due to accident, illness, professional liability, or theft. Your insurance needs will be determined largely by the type of consulting work you do, where your practice is located, and how your operation is run.

The following information should help to give you an idea of the kinds of insurance that are available.

Fire Insurance

Fire insurance protects your building and the property contained within it against damage inflicted by fire or lightning. Standard fire insurance policies do not cover accounting records, securities, deeds, money, bills, or manuscripts. Nor do they protect you against smoke and water damage that occurs as a result of a fire. To guard excluded valuables and protect against these exempted hazards, additional coverage is needed.

If your consulting practice is located in your home and you already have insurance, your existing policy may provide sufficient protection. Be sure to talk to your insurance agent, though, to determine if additional coverage is required. Standard homeowner's policies frequently exclude home-based businesses. In the case of convenience office and desk space arrangements, fire insurance is normally provided by the lessor. Check your lease agreement to verify this.

Automobile Insurance

If one or more automobiles or trucks will be used in your consulting practice, automobile insurance is a must. It protects you against property damage and bodily-injury claims as well as the actions of uninsured motorists.

The amount of coverage you need and the cost of a policy depend on the number of cars or trucks being insured, their value, the kinds of driving that they'll be used for (driving clients around, transporting materials and equipment), and your location.

Professional Liability Insurance

Any professional who provides advice or information to others or performs a service should seriously consider obtaining professional liability insurance. This protects consultants against damages claims resulting from mistakes they might make or their failure to complete an assignment. The most common type of professional liability insurance for consultants is errors and omissions insurance. Although the premium can be steep, you may be able to obtain it at a reduced rate by purchasing it through a professional group or association in which you are a member.

Personal Insurance

Personal insurance protects both you and your employees, if any, against personal loss. Health and life insurance, a retirement plan, and key personnel insurance all contribute to this protection. Key personnel insurance is particularly important if your consulting firm is a partnership or relies on the services of a key employee. In the event that the key person dies or is disabled, the proceeds from the policy are paid directly to the consulting firm.

Worker's Compensation

Employers are required by law to have worker's compensation insurance for their employees to cover damages arising from on-the-job injuries or occupational diseases. Thus, if you intend to employ others in your consulting practice, you will want to obtain this insurance.

Crime Insurance

To protect your property against thefts, you'll need some kind of crime insurance. The most popular form is the *comprehensive insurance policy.* A sort of all-in-one policy, this protects you not only against burglaries and robberies but a variety of other hazards as well.

CHOOSING A LEGAL FORM

Last, but not least, in setting up your consulting practice, you'll want to choose the legal form that best suits your needs. The three types from which to choose are the sole proprietorship, the partnership, and the corporation.

Sole Proprietorship

A consulting practice owned by one person, who is entitled to all of its profits and responsible for all of its debts, is considered a sole proprietorship. Providing maximum control and minimum government interference, this legal form is currently used by more than 75 percent of all businesses. The main advantages of the sole proprietorship are (1) the ease with which it can be started, (2) the owner's freedom to make decisions, and (3) the distribution of profits (owner takes all).

The sole proprietorship isn't without its disadvantages, though, the most serious of which is its unlimited liability. As a sole proprietor, you are responsible for all business debts. Should these exceed the assets of your consulting firm, your creditors can then claim your personal assets as well. Sole proprietorships also tend to have more difficulty obtaining capital and holding on to key employees. So any consultant who chooses to set up a sole proprietorship should be prepared to work independently, primarily drawing on his or her own resources.

Partnership

A consulting practice owned by two or more people, who agree to share its profits, is considered a partnership. Like the sole proprietorship, it is easy to start and the red tape involved is usually minimal. The main advantages of a partnership are that the consulting firm can (1) draw on the skills and abilities of each partner, (2) offer employees the chance to become partners, and (3) utilize the partners' combined financial resources.

But partnerships do have their share of disadvantages. The unlimited liability that applies to sole proprietorships is even worse for partnerships. As a partner in a consulting

THE ADVANTAGES AND DISADVANTAGES
OF EACH LEGAL FORM OF OWNERSHIP

Sole Proprietorship

Advantages	Disadvantages
1. You're the boss. 2. It's easy to get started. 3. You keep all profits. 4. Income from business is taxed as personal income. 5. You can discontinue your business at will.	1. You assume unlimited liability. 2. The investment capital you can raise is limited. 3. You need to be a generalist. 4. Retaining high-caliber employees is difficult. 5. The life of the business is limited.

Partnership

Advantages	Disadvantages
1. Two heads are better than one. 2. It's easy to get started. 3. More investment capital is available. 4. Partners pay only personal income tax. 5. High-caliber employees can be made partners.	1. Partners have unlimited liability. 2. Profits must be shared. 3. The partners may disagree. 4. The life of the business is limited.

Corporation

Advantages	Disadvantages
1. Stockholders have limited liability. 2. Corporations can raise the most investment capital. 3. The business has unlimited life. 4. Ownership is easily transferrable. 5. Corporations utilize specialists.	1. Corporations are taxed twice. 2. Corporations must pay capital stock tax. 3. Starting a corporation is expensive. 4. Corporations are more closely regulated.

firm, you are responsible not only for your own business debts but also for those of your partners. Should they incur debts or legal judgments against the consulting practice, you could be held legally responsible for them. Disputes among partners can also be a problem. Before entering into a partnership agreement, make sure that you and your partners see eye to eye on how the consulting practice should be run. (*Note:* for your own protection, you should have a *written* partnership agreement.)

Corporation

A corporation differs from the other legal forms of business in that the law regards it as an artificial being possessing the same rights and responsibilities as a person. Thus, unlike a sole proprietorship or partnership, it has an existence separate from its owners. As a result, the corporation offers some unique advantages. These include (1) limited liability (owners are not personally responsible for the debts of the business), (2) the option of raising capital by selling shares of stock, and (3) easy transfer of ownership from one individual to another. And, again unlike the sole proprietorship and partnership, the corporation has "unlimited life" and thus the potential to outlive its original owners.

The main disadvantages of the corporation can be summed up in two words: *taxation* and *complexity*. In what amounts to double taxation, you must pay taxes on both the income the corporation earns and the income (salary and dividends) you receive from the corporation. In addition, corporations are required to pay an annual tax on all outstanding shares of stock. Given its complexity, a corporation is both more difficult and more expensive to start than the other legal forms. You must obtain a charter from the state in which your consulting firm is located; this process usually requires the services of an attorney. The total cost of incorporating, including government and attorney fees, generally ranges from $500 to $1,500.

One way to have the advantages of a corporation without

the tax disadvantages is to form an *S corporation*. This is a special type of corporation that the Internal Revenue Service permits to be taxed as a partnership rather than a corporation. In order to qualify for S corporation status, though, your consulting firm must meet the specific requirements set forth by the IRS.

4

Determining Your Consulting Fees

ONE OF THE most difficult decisions for new consultants is deciding what price to put on their services. If you set your fees too high, you run the risk of losing potential clients. If you set them too low, you will lose potential profits. Thus, in determining your fees, you want to arrive at a price that is satisfactory to both you and the client.

COMPUTING YOUR FEES

In order to compute your consulting fees accurately, you must have a thorough understanding of your own needs and those of the marketplace. The fee schedule that you ultimately decide upon should take into consideration five major factors: salary, overhead, profit, competition, and the economy.

Salary

The starting point in computing your consulting fees is your salary. In essence, your fees need to be sufficient to provide you with a salary equal to or better than what you could receive by working as an employee in someone else's business. What that salary will be depends partly on your own expectations and personal valuation of your worth to clients. It also depends on the current demand for your services. Highly skilled consultants in high-demand fields can and do command top fees that translate into top salaries. Equally skilled consultants in fields where there is less demand earn proportionally less because of the downward pressure on fees. On the plus side, consultants with relatively little experience—such as recent graduates—can often increase their earning power by focusing on high-demand fields.

If you are uncertain about what your salary should be, check with other consultants in your field to find out an appropriate salary range. Or check with the appropriate professional association; most keep annual statistics on the salary levels of their members. To find out which associations represent your consulting field, refer to the section on "Trade and Professional Associations" in Chapter 9.

Overhead

Overhead is usually defined as the ongoing costs of running a business. It includes, among other things, rent, utilities, telephone, insurance, pension, promotion, typing, photocopying, and travel expenses. *All* business expenses should go into computing your fees. In so far as consulting firms are concerned, overhead is broken down into two categories: (1) client-related expenses, and (2) general expenses. Client-related expenses are incurred on the client's behalf and are billed directly to the client's account *in addition to your consulting fee*. General expenses are incurred on behalf of your business and are absorbed by the business *through your fees*. The main difference between the two categories is that client-related expenses are fully reimbursable, whereas general expenses must be covered by the fees you charge. For more information on business expenses and how they pertain to your recordkeeping and taxes, see Chapter 12.

Profit

Some consultants set their fees high enough to cover their salary and overhead requirements but neglect to consider their profits. Either they don't realize the error or they believe that their profits are already included in their salaries. This is not the case. As an entrepreneur and risk-taker, you are entitled to receive a profit on top of your salary. This is justified by the fact that you are assuming more responsibility and exposing yourself to more risk than you would if you were merely an employee. Depending on the type of consulting work you do, your profit should be between 10 and 25 percent of your combined salary and overhead. If your services are unique and there is a high demand for them, your profit may exceed this range. To determine the amount of profit you should receive for your efforts, find out what's standard for your consulting field. You can obtain this information by talking to other consultants or by contacting the professional associations referred to earlier.

Competition

Your consulting firm doesn't exist in a vacuum. In computing your fees, you must also keep in mind what your competitors charge for similar services. This is particularly important whenever you are in a bidding situation where the contract to be awarded goes to the lowest qualified bidder. To get a better idea of the fee range for your type of consulting services, use any and all of these sources of information: other consultants, professional associations, former clients of consultants, business leaders in your community.

Once you have ascertained the acceptable fee range for the type and quality of services you are prepared to offer, you can set your fees accordingly, opting for the low, middle, or top portion of the range. Don't assume that by setting your fees at the lowest possible level, though, you will automatically get business. While this may be true in bidding situations, it isn't always true in other situations. A price that's too low can be as much of a turn-off to prospective clients as a price that's too high; low fees are often equated with low value or inferior services.

The Economy

A pricing strategy that fails to consider the state of the economy will be doomed from the start. In addition to reflecting your costs and the competition, your fees should also reflect the economic environment in which you operate. You must consider, for instance, any increases or decreases in interest rates, changes in the tax laws, the rate of inflation, employment trends, consumer spending and savings patterns, and productivity levels. When prospective clients are experiencing strong economic periods, fees alone are rarely the deciding factor in choosing a consultant. During weak economic periods, it's another matter. Given the need to reduce costs, clients are more inclined to comparison-shop, looking for those consultants whose fees match their budgets. To keep your fees in line with the economy, it's essential for you to be aware of the economic changes that are occurring and of their effect on your clients.

TYPES OF FEE ARRANGEMENTS

Depending on the nature of the consulting work you do or the individual requirements of particular assignments, you may opt to use one fee arrangement or another. Payments are most commonly made (1) according to an hourly rate, (2) on a per-project basis, (3) on a retainer agreement, (4) on a performance basis, or (5) on an equity basis.

Hourly Rate

Consultants and clients alike often favor using an hourly rate because of its versatility and simplicity. From the consultant's point of view, arriving at a fee is just a matter of multiplying the hours spent working for the client times the rate per hour. From the client's point of view, this arrangement eliminates the need to enter into a long-term agreement with the consultant or to pay for time not received. In situations where the client only requires services for a short period of time or on a sporadic basis, it's usually preferable to use the hourly rate.

Taking into account the factors described earlier, you can compute your hourly rate as shown here:

Salary per hour	$_____
(Your estimated worth)	
Overhead per hour	+ $_____
(Weekly total/40 hours)	
Profit per hour	+ $_____
(____% × [Salary + overhead])	
Total hourly rate	$_____

By inserting the appropriate dollar amounts on the salary, overhead, and profit lines and then adding them together, you will arrive at your total hourly rate.

Per-Project Basis

Setting your fee on a per-project basis differs from the hourly rate in that, instead of being paid for your expenditure of time, you will be paid a prearranged sum for your successful completion of a specific project. In this type of arrangement, the fee that you are to receive is estimated in advance and fixed at that amount. If the project turns out to require more time than you anticipated, your fee remains unchanged. Any increase in cost must be absorbed by you. Conversely, if the project takes less time than anticipated, you still receive the full amount of the fee originally agreed upon.

The per-project basis is best suited to situations where a specific task needs to be carried out, such as conducting a market research survey, designing a brochure, or delivering a presentation. By your estimating the fee in advance, the client knows what to expect and doesn't have to worry about mounting costs if the project gets out of hand. This method can be advantageous to you as well. It not only rewards you for your efficiency but also simplifies your billing procedures since it does away with the need to provide the client with a breakdown of how your time was spent. To use the per-project fee arrangement effectively, though, you must be able to determine accurately how much of your time each project will require.

Retainer Agreement

A retainer agreement is a fee arrangement in which a client agrees to pay a consultant a predetermined monthly fee over an extended period of time (usually six months to a year). In exchange, the consultant guarantees the client a minimum number of consulting hours per month, as needed. As you can see, a retainer agreement serves basically two purposes: (1) it assures the client of having access to the consultant's services, and (2) it provides the consultant with a steady cash flow.

Retainer agreements are usually advisable in situations where clients know they are going to need ongoing advice or assistance over a period of months. For instance, a client who needs help in developing a community-relations program, researching new markets, or analyzing investment opportunities would probably benefit from a retainer agreement. Essentially, the client eliminates any risk of your being unavailable by booking your services in advance. What's more, unlike the per-project fee arrangement, which is limited to one specific project, the retainer can cover a variety of consulting assignments over an extended period of time.

Performance Basis

A performance basis fee arrangement is one in which all or part of the payment you receive depends upon the quality of your performance or on the result you achieve for the client.

For instance, a client hiring a consultant to institute an improved system for collecting bad debts might agree to pay the consultant a percentage of the monies collected. A training consultant, who is brought in by a company to train newly hired employees, could receive a bonus for each employee who successfully completes the training program.

For this arrangement to work, though, two things are necessary. First, you must have the authority to implement your recommendations and/or carry out the activities connected with the assignment. Second, the criteria for evaluating your performance must be measurable (i.e., monies collected, number of employees trained). To avoid disagreements later, you should agree to consult on a performance basis only when both of these stipulations have been met.

Equity Basis

In some instances, a consultant may be asked to offer his or her services in exchange for ownership in the client's business. This type of arrangement most commonly occurs when a business is still in the early stages or when a business is facing bankruptcy. In both situations the client needs the consultant's services but is not in a position to pay for them. If you agree to work on an equity basis and the business succeeds, you stand to receive far more for your efforts than what your normal fees would have been. However, if the business fails, you could end up with nothing. Given the risk involved, equity basis fee arrangements should be entered into with extreme caution.

PAYMENT SCHEDULES

In addition to negotiating a fee arrangement with each client, you also need to establish a payment schedule specifying how and when you are to be paid for your work. For instance, a payment schedule might stipulate that you are to bill the client on a monthly basis, charging for your time (at a specified hourly rate) and any client-related expenses, such as travel and long-distance phone calls. Or, if you have agreed to work on a per-project basis and your total fee has already been determined, the payment schedule can stipulate the amount and timing of the payments you are to receive (i.e., equal payments of $4,000 due on February 1 and March 1).

Constructing a payment schedule that is mutually acceptable to you and the client isn't always easy. Ideally, the schedule you decide upon should benefit both parties, helping to protect your right to be paid and the client's right to the services you promised. At the same time, the payment schedule should consider the matter of cash flow. Here it is important to decide reasonably who should have use of the money while the consulting assignment is being performed. Obviously, you would prefer to receive full payment in advance before starting the assignment, since this gives you immediate use of the money and avoids any collection problems later. The client, on the other hand, wants to delay making payment until after the assignment is completed, thereby retaining use of the money and control over your work. To satisfy both of you, some form of compromise is needed.

Progress Payments

Most consultants find that the best way to resolve the payment issue is to ask for progress payments. Here, instead of receiving your total fee up front or after the assignment is over, you receive periodic payments at various stages throughout the assignment. Billing on a monthly basis, as described earlier, is a standard practice for assignments that are spread out over a number of months. Another widely used payment schedule, which we strongly recommend when possible, is to require *payment in thirds*. Under this arrangement, you are paid one-third of your total fee prior to starting the assignment. The second third is paid to you midway through the assignment. The final third is paid to you upon completion of the assignment or within thirty days thereafter. The advantage of this method is that it links the payments you receive to your output. Although you don't have to actually "do" anything to receive the first payment, this is regarded as "good-faith money" in that it proves the client's ability and willingness to pay for your services. If payment in thirds isn't feasible (either because a fixed fee hasn't been determined or because another payment schedule is more suitable), it's still a good idea to request part of your fee up front. This is particularly advisable when you haven't worked with the client before or you have doubts about the client's credit.

MAXIMIZING YOUR PROFITABILITY

Even consultants who are good at setting fees and establishing payment schedules can inadvertently let profits slip through their fingers. On paper it looks as though they are achieving their full profit potential, but in reality they are not. Why? Because certain mistakes, commonly made in conducting a consulting practice, are cutting into their profits. These mistakes include:

1. *Not charging for your advice.* Consultants often make the mistake of giving away their advice rather than selling it. This is most likely to occur when you are trying to convince a potential client to use your services. What usually happens in this instance is that the consultant, in an effort to demonstrate his or her abilities, provides too much information. Then, having in effect told the client everything already, the consultant's services are no longer needed.

2. *Providing additional services not included in your original agreement.* Once an assignment is underway, you may discover that there are more facets to it than you had realized. As a result, more work is required. An example is the marketing consultant who is hired to create a brand name for a new product and ends up designing the package, too. In this situation, rather than not doing the additional work or doing it at no extra charge, you should bring your findings to the client's attention. Then, if the client wants you

to perform the additional services, you can recalculate your fee to include them.

3. *Failing to bill the client for travel time.* Consultants have been known to spend four hours driving to and from a client's office and then to only bill the client for a one-hour meeting. One way to get around this type of situation is to have the client come to *your* office, thereby eliminating the time you would spend commuting. Another way is to establish a minimum fee for your services that includes your travel time.

4. *Not keeping track of client-related expenses.* Consultants rarely need to be reminded to keep a record of their air travel and hotel expenses while working on an assignment. But what about long-distance phone calls, postage, typing, photocopying, materials purchased, and more? These everyday expenses you incur on the client's behalf need to be accounted for in addition to your services. In order to have these expenses reimbursed by the client, you must keep detailed records (backed up by receipts) explaining why and when each expense was incurred.

5

Promoting the Business

IN ADDITION to performing your consulting duties, you should plan to spend part of your time actively promoting your business. Providing good service alone isn't enough. It's important for you to identify prospective clients and to develop an overall strategy for communicating with them.

The services provided by successful consulting firms often aren't any better than those provided by firms that are struggling. So what separates them? Why are some consulting firms generating healthy profits while others are barely getting by? Promotion makes the difference. The successful firms recognize the value of self-promotion and make it a point to keep prospective clients informed about what they have to offer. Rather than waiting for business to come to them, they go out to get it.

IDENTIFYING YOUR BEST PROSPECTS

In choosing your consulting field(s), no doubt you gave considerable thought to the kinds of people or institutions who would be most likely to need your services. Your next step is to build a client profile of your best prospects: the prospective clients who show the most promise of actually retaining you as a consultant.

Building a Client Profile

A prospect is any individual, business, or organization that might be able to utilize your consulting services. A good prospect, however, is much more. As shown in the following chart depicting your client profile, a good prospect has three characteristics: (1) a need for your services, (2) the ability to afford them, and (3) the authorization to buy them. If any one of these requirements is missing, you probably won't get the assignment. Or if you do, you may have difficulty in getting paid for your work later.

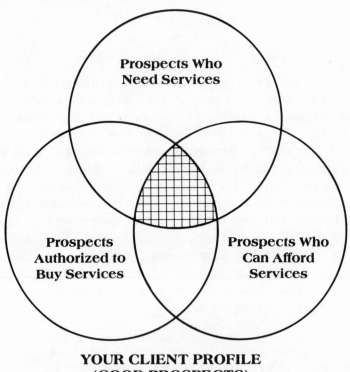

**YOUR CLIENT PROFILE
(GOOD PROSPECTS)**

Consultants, in particular, need to spend their time wisely. After all, time is your most valuable resource. Thus, you don't want to waste it trying to promote your business to bad prospects. The way to avoid this mistake is to ask yourself the following questions.

Does the Prospect Need My Services?

The most basic rule of business is "Find a need and fill it." Taking this into consideration, your first priority should be to determine if a prospect has a need for the types of consulting services you provide. Will using your services enable the prospective client to save or make money? Increase efficiency? Solve a problem? Look or feel better? Enjoy life more? Be more successful? The greater the prospect's need for your consulting services, the better your chance of winning the assignment. For instance, a catering consultant should focus on cultivating those businesses or individuals who entertain a lot. A financial planner would want to identify people within a certain tax bracket who are likely to need advice on sheltering and increasing their income.

Can the Prospect Afford My Services?

Ability to pay is an important criterion in judging whether or not a potential client is a good prospect. This is especially true in those situations where a major portion of your fee won't be due until *after* your work is completed. There's no point in promoting your services to a prospect who can't afford them. Much as the prospect might need what you have to offer, it's equally important that the client have sufficient funds to pay you. Otherwise you could succeed in getting the consulting assignment but have nothing more than a bad debt to show for it. If a prospect is unable to pay you yet you still feel committed to the project, you might proceed on an equity fee arrangement. Obviously, however, such an agreement entails more risk.

Is the Prospect Authorized to Buy My Services?

Just because a prospect needs and can afford your services doesn't mean that the prospect is authorized to hire you as a consultant. Someone else—a person or a committee—may be the party with the actual authority to enter into an agreement with you. All too often this detail is overlooked by consultants. In their eagerness to firm up an assignment, they assume that a prospect has more authority than is in fact true. For instance, a line supervisor in a factory may have a genuine need for the services of an air conditioning and heating specialist. What's more, the company can afford to hire such a person. But the authority to do so actually rests with a senior-level manager. In promoting your services to businesses, you'll find that the authority to buy can be spread out over several different departments and levels of management. Depending on the scope and cost of a consulting project, it's not uncommon for as many as a dozen or more people to have a say in the buying decision. As a rule of thumb, the higher up your contacts are in an organization's management structure, the easier it will be for you to get the approvals you need.

YOUR PROMOTIONAL STRATEGY

Having identified your best prospects, your goal is to get the word out about the types of consulting services you are prepared to offer them. What's needed here is a promotional strategy, or game plan, for communicating with those individuals depicted in your client profile. In essence, a promotional strategy is a selection process whereby you select the channels of communication that are best suited for reaching your audience. The various channels you have to choose from fall under one of three headings: networking, publicity, and advertising.

Networking refers to any form of personal communication you use to promote your business or yourself. It calls for you to establish and maintain a network of friends, colleagues, satisfied clients, and others who are good prospects for your consulting services or can help you to reach those who are. Frequently cited by consultants as their most effective promotional tool, networking is also one of the least expensive. It is time-consuming, however. In order to be successful, networking requires your personal involvement and the willingness to share information with the people in your network.

Publicity refers to any nonpaid form of mass communication you use to promote your business. It entails getting information about your consulting firm's services or activities reported in the news media. Such coverage is provided free of charge when the information is thought to have news value or to be of interest to the public. Publicity can be best characterized by its *three C's:* cost, control, and credibility. As indicated, there is no cost to you for the media coverage you receive. At the same time, however, you have no control over what the nature of that coverage will be. Publicity can be favorable or unfavorable—as likely to point out your consulting firm's mistakes as its accomplishments. If a news broadcast chooses to focus on a lawsuit that's been brought against you, rather than on the prestigious award you've just won, there's little you can do about it. It's this very lack of control, though, that gives publicity its greatest strength—credibility; when the news media, rather than a sponsor, delivers your message, it's much more believable.

Advertising refers to any *paid* form of mass communication you use to promote your business. In general, it involves the purchasing of print space or air time in various communication media, such as magazines and radio. Though recognized as a necessary business communication tool, the role of advertising in promoting consulting firms is less clear. Consultants often believe that they don't need to advertise or that they *shouldn't* advertise. Some consider it demeaning to their professional image. Others are afraid that their clients will find it offensive. But when used properly, advertising produces positive results. A consulting firm has as much to gain from skillful advertising as does any other business. Unlike networking or publicity, advertising is the only communication method that gives you total control over the information that is directed at your audience.

Which Method Should You Use?

Which should you use—networking, publicity, or advertising? The answer is: all three. For your promotional strategy to be really effective, you should use the channels of communication within each of these categories. A consultant whose promotional strategy relies on networking alone will be unable to reach contacts outside his or her present network. Relying too heavily on publicity to communicate with prospective clients will result in a promotional strategy that's lacking in continuity and control. And if you use only advertising, you will be missing out on the opportunity to meet prospective clients firsthand or to get free media exposure for your consulting practice. Networking expands your personal contacts. Publicity helps to build your reputation. Advertising provides control and a sense of direction.

NETWORKING, PUBLICITY, AND ADVERTISING

The chart opposite shows the networking, publicity, and advertising methods you can use to promote your consulting practice. Depending on the types of consulting you do, your audience, and the money available for promotion, some methods will be more suitable than others.

Networking

The networking methods that follow should help you to make contact with prospects for your consulting services. Some of these methods can also be used to generate publicity.

Phone Calls

AT&T's advice to "reach out and touch someone" has particular relevance for consultants. Using the telephone to strengthen existing relationships and to establish new ones is one of the best ways to promote your business. When you come across information that might be of value to someone in your network (or someone you would *like* to have in your network), call that person. Letting others know that you have their best interests in mind and are familiar with their concerns often leads to future consulting assignments.

NETWORKING, PUBLICITY, AND ADVERTISING

Networking

Phone Calls
Letters
Membership in Associations
Speeches and Seminars
Civic and Social Events

Publicity

Media Interviews
Published Articles
Newsletters
Books
Awards
Charitable Donations
Timely Event

Advertising

Yellow Pages
Direct Mail
Directory Listings
Newspapers
Magazines
Radio
Television
Sales Promotion
    Business Cards
    Brochures
    Advertising Specialty Items
    Trade Shows

Letters

Letters perform much the same promotional function as phone calls, but they allow you to send more detailed information. We frequently send out newspaper clippings, reports, and other materials we think will be of interest to the recipients. Although this takes time, the response (and additions to our client list) has been well worth our efforts.

Membership in Associations

There's no substitute for actually meeting the leaders in your particular industry or profession and having the opportunity to exchange ideas and information. Associations make this possible, bringing people together and providing forums for discussion. To take full advantage, find out which professional or trade associations best serve your needs, and then plan to join at least one. It's also a good idea to join a group where you can meet people in fields outside your own, such as the Chamber of Commerce, Rotary Club, or Women in Business.

Speeches and Seminars

Attending a speech or seminar enables you to accomplish two things at once: to gain additional information and to make new contacts. Taking this one step further, though, why not give speeches or conduct seminars yourself? This can be an extremely effective tool for promoting your consulting services and enhancing your reputation as an expert in your field. To achieve the best results, try to determine which topics hold the greatest interest for the people you want to reach. And whenever you give a speech or conduct a seminar, make it a point to get the names and addresses of those in attendance. In addition, by notifying the press of an upcoming speaking engagement or seminar, you should be able to obtain media coverage as well. For more information about using speeches and seminars to generate additional income, see Chapter 11.

Civic and Social Events

These gatherings provide still another avenue for developing client leads. One of the advantages of this method of networking is that it enables you to meet people who ordinarily would be difficult to reach or inaccessible. And since the environment itself is a more relaxing one, conversation is relatively easy. Don't make the mistake, though, of trying to deliver your sales presentation then and there when you meet someone who appears to be a good prospect. This is generally considered in poor taste at nonbusiness events. Instead, follow up the meeting with a phone call or letter inviting further discussion.

Publicity

The following publicity methods can be used to obtain media exposure for your business. In deciding which ones to use, pick those that are most compatible with your own abilities and personal preferences.

Media Interviews

The media frequently turn to outside experts for advice and information when putting together radio and television talk shows or researching newspaper and magazine articles. Making yourself available for media interviews is a way to reach thousands or even millions of people. The more relevant your information is to a program's or publication's audience, the better your chance of being interviewed. The trick is to anticipate what an audience wants to know and then adapt your information accordingly. For instance, suppose you were a banking consultant interested in being interviewed by a well-known business publication or in appearing on a daytime television talk show. In approaching the business publication, you could stress your knowledge of current banking trends and the reasons behind recent interest rate fluctuations. The talk show, on the other hand, given its high percentage of women viewers, might prefer information on the specific credit laws that protect women.

Published Articles

Writing newspaper and magazine articles on subjects within your area of expertise is another way to get public recognition. If a newspaper or magazine thinks highly enough of your views to publish them, readers are assured that you must be an expert in your field. To really capitalize on this type of publicity, you should write for those publications whose readers are good prospects for your services. And don't spread yourself too thin. Consultants who try to be experts in several fields quickly lose their credibility. An investment consultant who is known for writing articles on the securities market shouldn't write about physical fitness . . . unless it's "Wall Street Reacts to the Physical-Fitness Craze." To find out more about getting published and how articles can also be a source of income, read Chapter 11.

Newsletters

Another way to reach prospective clients and gain the attention of the media is to publish your own newsletter. It should consist of four to eight pages and be published on a monthly, bimonthly, or quarterly basis. The information it contains should be timely and of use to those who will receive it. Your first goal is to use the newsletter to maintain contact with prospects for your consulting services. The second is to use it to increase your media coverage; through its distribution, you may be quoted or even interviewed. Besides publicity, newsletters can also generate additional income. For more information, see Chapter 11.

Books

Writing a book demands a much greater investment of your time than writing an article or publishing a newsletter, but the publicity value can be enormous. As a published author, you become more attractive to the media simply because the book can certify your expert status. And publishing a book increases your chance of being quoted or interviewed. The closer the subject is to your areas of specialization, the better. Ideally, many of the same people who read the book will also contact you regarding consulting assignments. See Chapter 11 for more information on books and how they can add to your income.

Awards

Winning an award can result in publicity too, since it lets others know that you have done something special which warranted recognition. Awards are generally given on the basis of professional achievements or volunteer service to the community. While there's no guarantee you will win an award, you *can* shift the odds in your favor. Entering awards contests sponsored by professional associations in your field is one way. Becoming an active participant in a civic or charitable group is another.

Charitable Donations

Donating your consulting services to a worthy cause is one of the nicest ways to get publicity. The people who receive your services benefit, and so do you. For instance, a career guidance consultant might help high school students to chart their career paths. A nutritionist could show senior citizens how to prepare simple, inexpensive, nourishing meals. These are the types of newsworthy stories that especially appeal to local newspapers and television news programs.

Timely Event

A promotional method often used with success by businesses is linking their publicity efforts to a timely event. Christmas, the World Series, even Tax Day can be used. The more creative your approach, the better. One investment counselor we know of gets extensive media coverage every Christmas. Each year he sends out a press release with his estimates of what it would cost, in current dollars, to buy all the gifts included in the song "The Twelve Days of Christmas." A special-effects make-up expert in the motion picture industry uses Halloween to its best advantage by demonstrating his talents on the five o'clock news to show how movie monsters are made.

Advertising

Each of the following advertising methods has its strengths and limitations. In choosing one medium or another, try to determine which one will enable you to reach your audience most effectively.

Yellow Pages

Any business that has a telephone is entitled to a free listing in the Yellow Pages section of the telephone book. In addition to this, for greater visibility, you may also want to purchase a display ad to promote your services. Some consultants, such as graphic designers, real estate appraisers, catering consultants, and insurance specialists, use this method with great success. Others, however, claim that the results don't justify the expense. For instance, management consultants, attorneys, accountants, and others who frequently get their clients through referrals, usually do not fare as well with Yellow Pages advertising. In our own case, we found that while we got more telephone calls because of the Yellow Pages, few of the calls actually resulted in consulting assignments. More often than not the callers wanted to sell us *their* services or had us confused with some other type of consultant in a different field.

The main advantage of Yellow Pages advertising is its ability to reach people within a certain geographic area at the time when they want to buy. Having already recognized a need for a particular product or service, they are just looking for the right place to buy it. Thus, given the "pre-sold" nature of its audience, an ad in the Yellow Pages is essentially an attention-getting device. Your purpose is not only to provide information about the type of consulting work you do but also to differentiate yourself from the competition. Here it's important to emphasize what sets you apart from other consultants in your field—experience, resources and capabilities, awards won, or whatever.

Direct Mail

This form of advertising involves printed material, such as a letter or brochure, that is mailed directly to your prospective clients. Chief among direct mail's strengths are its selectivity and flexibility. These enable you to send any promotional message to anyone at any time. In addition, direct mail provides one of the best means of explaining and describing what your consulting firm does. For example, you can use direct mail to:

• Maintain client contact
• Reach new clients
• Develop your image
• Introduce new consulting services

Direct mail does have one serious limitation, however. If you aren't careful, the people who receive your materials may regard them as junk mail and throw them away. Thus, your primary concern in using direct mail should be to get your advertisement into the right hands. One point on which all marketing experts agree is that the success of any direct-mail campaign rests largely on the quality of its mailing list. The better your mailing list, the better the response to your advertisement.

You can either build your own mailing list or buy one from a list broker. If you decide to build the list yourself, some of the sources you can use include: present clients, client leads you have received, business cards, organization directories, public announcements, and government records. For information on list brokers, check the "Standard Rate and Data Service," a monthly publication available at many libraries. This directory will tell you which companies specialize in preparing the type of mailing list you need.

Directory Listings

A number of publishing companies and trade and professional associations print directories that contain listings of various types of consultants. For instance, there are directories that list consultants in such fields as financial planning, advertising, interior design, management, and banking. Thus, it may be possible to have information about your consulting firm and its capabilities included in one or more directories. When a directory is published by a trade or professional association, the listings in it are usually provided free of charge to members. Nonmembers are either excluded from the directory or required to pay a fee to obtain a listing. When a publishing company compiles and distributes a directory, you may or may not have to pay a fee to be included.

If you are contemplating obtaining a directory listing, first determine what the fee, if any, will be for it. Second, find out how many copies of the directory will be printed and who will receive them. After all, there's no benefit in being listed in a directory that no one will see. Ideally, the people who subscribe to the directory should be your prospective clients.

Newspapers

Approximately 30 percent of all advertising dollars spent in the United States goes toward newspaper advertising. Part of the appeal of newspapers is that their advertising rates are generally low and they are one of the most effective ways of reaching a local audience. And newspapers tend to have an upscale readership. Researchers have found that people who read newspapers are usually better educated and earn higher incomes than those who don't.

Just placing your ad in the newspaper, though, is no guarantee that your intended audience will read it. Readers frequently jump from one page to the next, merely glancing at ads or skipping them altogether. To catch someone's eye, it's essential to position your ad in a way to increase its exposure and heighten its effectiveness. Known as *preferred positioning*, this technique entails placing your ad in the section of the newspaper that is most often read by your prospective clients. For instance, a catering consultant might place an ad in either the food section or the entertainment section. A computer consultant could specify the business section. Another positioning tip recommended by advertising experts is to place your ad on a right-hand page whenever possible, preferably above the fold. This way more people will actually notice it.

Magazines

The main advantage of magazines as a promotional vehicle is their selectivity. Given the large number of special-interest, trade, and professional magazines available, there's practically one for every audience. By choosing the magazines that most appeal to your prospective clients, you're virtually assured of getting your message across to the right people. And since people frequently save magazines for future reference after they've read them, magazine ads tend to have a long life span.

On the down side, though, magazines have what's known as a long *lead time*—the interval between the time your ad is placed and the date it actually appears. Magazine ads usually must be received two or three months prior to publication. And, just as with newspapers, positioning is important. Otherwise your ad could be easily overlooked.

To find out which magazines reach your prospective clients, check the "Standard Rate and Data Service" publications described earlier. This will provide information about each magazine's readership and advertising rates.

Radio

Radio, though not one of the more popular advertising methods among consultants, shouldn't be ignored entirely. For one thing, it is the most pervasive of the media, able to reach people wherever they are, whatever they are doing. At home, work, driving in the car, or on vacation, people have their radios with them. In the United States today, there are almost two radios per person, with 99 percent of all households having at least one radio.

Like magazines, radio also offers a high degree of selectivity, since different stations and programs appeal to different audiences. Financial planners and accountants, for example, can reach prospective clients by advertising on radio programs devoted to business and financial news. Personnel consultants, on the other hand, might purchase air time on the kind of "easy listening" stations that are frequently broadcast in office buildings.

The main drawbacks to radio advertising are the costs and complexity of the medium. To be effective, a commercial must be broadcast repeatedly over a period of weeks or months. This repetition can be expensive. As for the complexity, putting together an effective commercial usually requires professional assistance. Fortunately, though, many radio stations make this assistance available to advertisers at little or no charge. And by advertising on smaller stations— mainly, the FM stations—you should be able to minimize your costs, since their rates are lower than those of the big stations.

Television

Little need be said about the impact television has on an audience or its ability to shape attitudes and change opinions. Currently, 98 percent of all American households have one or more television sets, and the average family watches TV for almost seven hours per day. Top-rated programs can and do reach upward of forty million viewers week after week.

The numbers are attractive. But along with the large numbers come television's high advertising rates. Television, like radio, is known for its cost and complexity. Most consultants would be hard-pressed to pay the price to advertise on network television. *Local television* and *cable television* are another matter, however. Many consultants are discovering that these are viable and affordable alternatives for promoting their businesses. Besides charging considerably lower rates than network television, local and cable TV offer advertisers a greater degree of selectivity in reaching prospective clients. To find out more about advertising on local or cable television and whether or not this meets your needs and budget, check the "Standard Rate and Data Service" publications.

Sales Promotion

Sales promotion is generally regarded as a supplement to advertising and includes such diverse promotional methods as business cards, brochures, advertising specialty items, and participation in trade shows.

Business Cards. Your business cards can be a strong promotional tool, defining the nature of your consulting services and enabling prospective clients to contact you. Properly wording the information on your cards will increase their effectiveness. So will choosing a card design that suits your image. Some consultants use business cards that are actually miniphotographs depicting themselves in action or surrounded by the tools of their trade. A banking consultant might be shown inside a bank vault surrounded by money, an import-export specialist standing on the dock next to a shipment of merchandise. These cards cost a bit more, but if they get results, the added expense is justified.

Brochures. In some businesses a brochure outlining your capabilities, accomplishments, and background is essential. It helps to legitimize your consulting practice and gives prospective clients something to refer to in evaluating whether or not to retain your services. Usually an $8\frac{1}{2} \times 11''$ sheet of quality paper, folded in thirds and printed on both sides, should do the job. After you've determined what to include in the brochure (a description of your services, biographical information, partial client list, and so on), check with several printers to find out what each would charge to print the quantity you need.

Advertising Specialty Items. An advertising specialty item is any object imprinted with your consulting firm's name and phone number on it and given to prospective clients. The most common types of specialty items are pens, pencils, memo pads, and key chains. Ideally, the item should be inexpensive, useful, and in keeping with your image. For example, engineering consultants might give out metric conversion tables. A wardrobe planner could give prospective clients small travel sewing kits.

Trade Shows. Purchasing exhibit space at trade shows, conventions, and conferences is another way to reach prospective clients. Consultants whose services are directed at specific industries (construction, transportation, and insurance, for instance) can use industry trade shows to communicate with decision-makers in these fields. Business development conferences also frequently prove to be good sources of client leads, particularly for consultants in such areas as data processing, direct mail, and sales training.

6

Meeting with Clients

THE WAY you conduct yourself in meetings will have a direct bearing on your ability to win and retain clients. Meetings are an integral part of consulting. They provide consultants and clients with the opportunity to come face-to-face with each other, to ask questions, exchange information, and to explore and develop positive working relationships. As such, the time you put into preparing for and participating in meetings should be regarded as time well spent.

To use meetings to their best advantage will require all of your skills, both as a consultant and as a communicator. In addition to demonstrating your knowledge and expertise, you must also show clients that you understand their problems and genuinely want to help solve them. Granted, turning prospects into clients isn't easy. Nor is it easy to keep current clients satisfied. However, you stand a better chance of accomplishing these goals once you learn how to make meetings work for you.

You should know about the different types of meetings that can take place, how to create a professional image, and what you can do to communicate most effectively and establish a good rapport with clients.

TYPES OF MEETINGS

As a consultant, you are likely to find yourself involved in networking meetings, initial consultations, formal presentations, updating meetings, summary meetings, and follow-up meetings.

Networking Meeting

Networking meetings are for the purpose of maintaining current business relationships or establishing contact with prospective clients. Unlike the other types of meetings, they are relatively unstructured and usually take place in a relaxed atmosphere, such as a restaurant. Or they may occur in conjunction with an event sponsored by a trade or professional association—at a convention or conference. During a networking meeting, any overt selling or demonstrating of your consulting services should usually be minimal. Your main goal is to find out about the activities in which the person you are meeting is presently involved and to develop any client leads that you can follow up later.

Initial Consultation

An initial consultation is when a consultant and a prospective (or new) client have their first formal meeting. It is normally scheduled by appointment and can take place in your office or the client's. The meeting's purpose is generally of an exploratory nature, to determine the extent of the client's needs and the role that you, as the consultant, might have in fulfilling those needs. Here, it is not only acceptable for you to try to sell the client on your consulting services; it is *expected.* Depending on the outcome of this meeting, you may be (1) retained as a consultant, (2) asked to prepare a formal presentation and/or proposal outlining the services you are qualified to provide, or (3) told that the client is unable to make a decision at this time.

Formal Presentation

The more complex a situation is, or the more people who are involved in the hiring decision, the more likely it is that you will be requested to give a formal presentation. During a formal presentation, clients want to see specifics. You will be expected, at the very least, to answer these questions: What do you intend to do? How long will it take you to complete the assignment? What will you accomplish? How much will your services cost?

Visual aids, samples of your work, statistics, case histories of similar assignments you have performed, and other such evidence of your expertise can come into play here. For example, it's standard for advertising consultants to bring samples of the ads they have helped to create. Risk management consultants, on the other hand, would probably rely on statistics to show how they can reduce the number of accidents and lower insurance premiums. In addition to the presentation itself, you may also be called upon to submit a detailed, written proposal explaining your approach to the situation. For more information on proposals, see Chapter 7.

Updating Meeting

The purpose of updating meetings is to keep the client informed of your progress once you have started work on an assignment. During an updating meeting, you can describe what you have already accomplished and explain what you plan to do next. This is also the time to ask or answer any questions that may arise. Depending on the terms of your agreement and the duration of the assignment, the number of updating meetings that take place can vary. In some instances, you may not need to schedule any meetings. In others, especially when the assignment is a lengthy one, you might schedule several meetings spread out over a period of months.

Summary Meeting

At the concusion of an assignment, it's often helpful to have a summary meeting with the client. This provides an opportunity for you to submit any remaining work or information that is due and for the client to ask questions. Based on the complexity of the assignment and what still needs to be discussed, a summary meeting can last anywhere from an hour to several days. The format of the meeting itself can range from a casual discussion over lunch to an elaborate presentation with audiovisuals. Although a summary meeting signifies the end of an assignment, successful consultants often are able to use the meeting as a springboard to future assignments. To do this, you must listen carefully to what the client is saying and try to read between the lines to detect any additional needs the client may still have.

Follow-Up Meeting

Follow-up meetings generally take place two to four weeks after an assignment has been completed. Here your goal is to let the client know that you stand behind the consulting services you provide. Rather than walking away from a completed assignment, you are interested in obtaining the client's feedback and are willing to offer additional assistance if it is needed. It's true that follow-up meetings require more of your time without any guarantee of increased revenues. But they go a long way toward satisfying clients and, in so doing, help to generate repeat business and client referrals.

Each type of meeting just described involves the exchange of a specific kind of information and serves its own unique purpose. Some consulting assignments will include all six types of meetings. Other assignments may call for only some of the meetings. In theory, each type of meeting should dovetail into the next. Of course, it won't always happen this way. Not all networking meetings result in actual consulting assignments. Nor will all assignments require formal presentations or updating meetings. Instead of arranging a follow-up meeting to obtain the client's feedback, you may prefer to make a phone call or write a letter. Whatever the situation, though, the greater your awareness of how and when to use the various types of meetings, the better equipped you will be to profit from them.

CREATING A PROFESSIONAL IMAGE

Given the personal nature of consulting work—*you* are the business—it's extremely important to define and cultivate your professional image. Not only must the image you decide upon match the expectations of your clients, but it must be compatible with your personality as well. The type of professional image that's suitable for a graphic designer differs from the image that's suitable for a tax consultant. The graphic designer needs to project an image that tells clients, "I possess the originality, creativity, and artistic skills necessary to get the job done. You are going to love my work." The tax consultant, on the other hand, needs a professional image that says, "Don't worry. I know the tax laws inside and out and I can save you money. Trust me."

The professional image you project to others is actually a combination of four separate components: words, actions, appearance, and environment.

Words

The words you use to address clients and to describe your consulting services, along with your tone of voice, all add to your professional image. Through your choice of words you can increase your credibility as an expert in your field and can help to put clients at ease. To achieve these ends, always make it a point to speak to clients with courtesy and respect. In discussing your work, explain the relevant details clearly and concisely, providing clients with an opportunity to ask questions. And, rather than trying to razzle-dazzle clients with recitations of your abilities, give your accomplishments a chance to speak for themselves.

Actions

Your actions can serve as a bridge to bring you and the client closer together or as a barrier to keep you apart. In your effort to present yourself as a professional, don't make the mistake of acting aloof or condescending. Successful consultants feel confident enough to treat clients as equals. At the same time, they always take the client's needs into consideration. For example, if a meeting is set to take place in your office, have all the materials you will need at hand so you won't have to waste the client's time looking for them. Then, before you begin to talk business, make sure that the client is comfortable. Offering coffee or tea is a nice gesture. Providing pens and paper for the client to take notes is another. By these actions and others, you not only show your concern for the client but demonstrate your competence and sense of control.

Appearance

Appearance is another facet of your professional image. Your attire and grooming tell clients a great deal about you, making a statement about your personality and even the quality of your consulting services. Despite warnings that it's wrong to judge a book by its cover, this is precisely what people do. First impressions *are* important. The more closely your appearance conforms to clients' expectations of how a successful consultant should look, the easier it will be for you to gain their confidence.

This isn't to say that there is only one look that is acceptable for consultants or that you shouldn't be allowed to express your personal taste and preferences in fashion. To achieve the right effect, you should adopt a style that is acceptable to you and the client. In comparing the appearance of the graphic designer and the tax consultant, mentioned earlier, two very different looks are likely to emerge. The graphic designer's clothing and accessories should convey a feeling of innovativeness and flair, whereas the tax consultant's attire should be more traditional, suggesting fiscal responsibility and good business sense.

Environment

Your work environment itself is also part of your professional image. Something as simple and basic as a desk can send a message to clients about the type of person you are and how you will approach a consulting assignment. For example, two desks of equal value—one constructed out of chrome and glass, the other made of dark mahogany—can present very different images. The first conveys a futuristic feeling and says that the owner is unconventional and an original thinker—the perfect image for the graphic designer. The second evokes a feeling of permanence and says that the owner is responsible and practical—not a bad image for the tax consultant. Depending on the other furnishings that surround each desk, these images can be reinforced or modified. Thus, the starkness of the chrome and glass can be softened by the addition of a comfortable sofa nearby. Any stodginess associated with the mahogany desk might be downplayed by hanging a modern painting on the wall. Whatever your environment, whether it's functional or formal, high-tech or traditional, you want it to help facilitate your relationship with clients. Rather than drawing attention to itself, it should serve as a backdrop for you, enhancing your professional image and adding to your credibility as a consultant.

COMMUNICATING EFFECTIVELY

The basis for establishing a rewarding consultant-client relationship ultimately comes down to one thing—communication. In order to work together, you and the client must be able to communicate with each other.

The suggestions that follow should help you to communicate more effectively with clients and strengthen your ability to promote and provide your consulting services.

1. *Put yourself in the client's position.* Good communicators know the importance of empathy–being able to see a situation from the other person's point of view. Granted, the

client has come to you for your ideas and perspective. But without first gaining an understanding of how the client perceives the situation, you can't begin to establish a dialog. To communicate more effectively, you should approach new client relationships with an open mind, putting preconceptions behind and allowing each client to tell his or her story.

2. *Don't overlook the nonverbal messages you are sending.* Your words may be saying one thing, but your body language (facial expressions, posture, gestures) may be saying something entirely different. For example, slouching in your chair while telling a client about your attention to detail and insistence on quality negates what you are saying. Avoiding the client's eyes after you've quoted your fee also sends a message—that the fee is too high or you haven't told the client everything. Tapping your fingers on a desk surface tells clients you are impatient. Shuffling papers usually indicates nervousness.

3. *Remember that the communication process is two-sided.* In addition to being a good speaker, you must also be a good listener. Once the client has received your input, it's up to you to interpret the feedback that is generated. Is the client's response to what you have just said positive or negative? Undecided? Is additional information needed? What doubts or uncertainties still exist? The better you are at interpreting and responding to the client's feedback, whether it's verbal or nonverbal, the better you will be at convincing the client of your views.

4. *Ask questions.* As the consultant, you expect the client to ask you questions, but what about the opposite? Answering questions is only half of your role. To obtain a thorough understanding of the client's situation, you must also be able to *ask* questions. Known as "probing," this entails getting clients to open up and reveal the types of information you need in order to carry out your assignment. You will find that probing helps you not only to get at the facts of the matter but also to develop a rapport with the client by emphasizing the collegial aspects of your relationship.

5. *Think before you speak.* During meetings or phone conversations with the clients, avoid the urge to "shoot from the

lip." It's better to tell a client that you need additional time to check your facts or gather the necessary information than to give an inaccurate or incomplete answer. The same applies to making suggestions or identifying any problems that may exist. Here you should resist the temptation to give on-the-spot, instant analyses of situations before you have had a chance to formulate your thoughts and weigh the various alternatives. The ability to think and act quickly is an asset, but so is having the patience to do an assignment correctly.

6. *Be enthusiastic.* If you aren't enthusiastic about your consulting services, why should the client be? In communicating with the client, it's important for you to get the point across that you enjoy your work and are eager to use your abilities on the client's behalf. This doesn't mean resorting to phoniness or hype, but simply showing the client that you will tackle the assignment with the energy and enthusiasm it deserves.

7. *Personalize the relationship.* Address clients by their names, rather than constantly referring to them as "you." When personal information is revealed, such as a client's hobbies, plans for an upcoming trip, or details about family members, make a mental note of it so you can refer to it at a later date. This lets clients know that you value them as individuals and not just "accounts."

8. *Be prepared.* The Boy Scouts' motto has as much relevance for consultants as it does for scouts. In order to communicate effectively, you must have something to say. You should do your research in advance and have access to the materials and information you will need to get your points across and to answer the client's questions. Few things can be more damaging to the consultant-client relationship than showing up for meetings unprepared or failing to anticipate the client's concerns. The key word here is "anticipate." In addition to reacting to the client's current needs, you should try to foresee any new ones on the horizon and be prepared to satisfy them.

9. *Whenever possible, provide tangible proof of what you can do.* In addition to the usual facts and figures, it helps to appeal to

the client's five senses—the ability to hear, see, touch, smell and taste. Food-related services are a natural for this technique. For example, catering consultants shouldn't just describe the various dishes they prepare but should show color photographs of them attractively displayed . . . or, better yet, offer clients samples to taste. With a little imagination, other types of consulting services can also be made to appeal to the senses. Sales-training consultants can demonstrate their abilities by showing prospective clients videocassettes of their training sessions. Computer consultants can use the hands-on approach by getting clients to sit at the computer and actually operate it.

10. *Emphasize benefits, rather than features.* Whereas features describe your consulting services, benefits are the advantage the client will derive from using them. The essential difference, as shown in the following examples, is that benefits give the client a reason to buy.

FEATURES	BENEFITS
Our firm specializes in office design and layout.	Changing your layout will increase employee morale and productivity.
I advise clients on the computers and software that are available.	I will select and install the best computer system for your needs.
This physical-fitness program includes instruction in both diet and exercise.	After completing the program, you'll see a noticeable improvement in your stamina and appearance.
I provide companies with government marketing information.	I will show you how you can win government contracts.
My public relations firm represents several major corporations.	I can get your company the media exposure it deserves.

(continued on next page)

FEATURES	BENEFITS
I'll examine all aspects of your credit and collection procedures.	In similar situations, I've improved clients' collection rates by up to 30 percent.
As a catering consultant, I know what goes into planning a dinner party.	Your dinner party will be a huge success.
We'll set up and monitor your inventory control system.	Inventory shortages and surpluses will be a thing of the past.

As you can see, instead of focusing on what your services are, you want to communicate what your services can do for the client.

7

Preparing Proposals, Contracts, and Reports

PROPOSALS, contracts, and reports are the tools of the consultant's trade. They enable you to package and present your services, define the terms of your agreements, and apprise clients of your progress. By developing the ability to express yourself through these written materials, you can work more harmoniously with clients and enhance your standing as a consultant.

PROPOSALS THAT SELL

Before entering into an agreement, more often than not, clients will want you to prepare a proposal explaining the consulting services you wish to provide. The purpose of such a proposal is twofold: (1) it provides the client with the necessary information to reach a decision, and (2) it serves as a vehicle for promoting your services. To achieve the best results, your proposals should:

- Define the client's situation as you see it, emphasizing the problems that need to be solved or actions that need to be taken.
- Outline the steps you would take to remedy the situation.

- Establish yourself as the person most qualified to carry out the assignment.
- Highlight the benefit to be derived from utilizing your services.

Based on your understanding of the client's needs and budget, your proposal may be quite detailed, going so far as to specify how and when the work would be completed, what your fees and payment schedule would be. In this instance, your proposal closely resembles a letter of agreement, and in fact, if both parties sign it, the proposal can become a binding contract. When you have only a general idea of what the client wants, though, your proposal should be less specific, describing your consulting services in broader terms. Later, once you and the client have clarified the situation, you can expand your original proposal or incorporate the additional information into a written contract.

What to Put in Your Proposal

Part of the secret to writing proposals is to make them as "reader friendly" as possible. You should anticipate the reader's questions and concerns, and supply the appropriate specifics to answer them. Your proposal should also be well organized and professional in appearance. As for the length of a proposal, this can vary in accordance with the size and dollar value of the project. The more involved a project is, the more the reader usually expects to see. Proposals for major government projects are sometimes hundreds of pages long. However, this is the exception, rather than the rule. The majority of proposals for consulting projects range from one to three pages in length to a maximum of twenty-five pages.

To make your proposals more acceptable to prospective clients, it helps to include certain key elements in your proposal format. Depending on the nature of the consulting project itself, your proposal should contain some or all of the following elements:

Letter of transmittal. A letter of transmittal, or cover letter, should always accompany your proposal even if one isn't specifically requested as part of the proposal package. This letter serves to introduce you to the prospective client and to identify your proposal.

Title page. This states the topic of your proposal and provides such information as: your name and/or company's name, your address and phone number, and the date the proposal was prepared. If the proposal is in response to a government Request For Proposals (RFP), additional information may be needed here to identify the RFP to which your proposal pertains.

Table of contents. The value of a table of contents is that it tells the reader at a glance what information is included in your proposal and where to find it. Rather than having to hunt for the desired information, it is readily accessible. On short proposals of three pages or less, the table of contents is unnecessary. On longer proposals it is essential.

Summary of the proposal. This section, consisting of one to two paragraphs, describes what you intend to do. It should be brief and to the point, defining the consulting project and its overall purpose.

What the proposal will accomplish. Taking your summary one step further, this section focuses on the benefits the client will receive once your proposal has been carried out. Such benefits may include: increased efficiency, cost savings, improved employee morale, the achievement of an objective, and so on. Stating the benefits in this way makes your proposal more saleable, but be careful not to promise more than you can deliver.

Scope of the work. This section is the real "nuts and bolts" of your proposal. It sets forth the proposed processes and specific tasks needed to meet the objectives of the consulting project. Your approach to the assignment and the methodology you would employ should be carefully explained. Note that you don't need to give away any trade secrets or proprietary information here but that the information you provide must be specific enough so that the client knows what your work will entail.

Estimated time required. Based on your knowledge of the

consulting project, estimate how long it will take to complete the various tasks involved. The more you know about the project itself and the client's needs, the more specific you can be. As a rule of thumb, give yourself some leeway—a margin of 10 percent or so—in calculating the project's time span. That way, if everything doesn't go according to plan, you still have time to take corrective action.

Estimated cost. As was the case with your time estimate, the more you know about the project, the more closely you can estimate its cost. If your proposal is primarily an exploratory one and many of the details have yet to be resolved, then you should not attempt to estimate costs at this time. To do so would not only result in an estimate of questionable accuracy but might alienate the client. On the other hand, if the client is requesting bids or if the issue of costs has already been clarified, then try to be as specific as you can. At the same time, you should explain how client-related expenses are to be handled and what your billing procedures are.

Qualifications and experience. In this section you should outline the qualifications and experience that make you suited to perform the proposed assignment. Citing specific education or training that you may have, similar projects successfully completed, or experience gained while working for a former employer should help to bolster your position. Background information should also be provided for any associates or subcontractors you intend to use in the project.

Adhering to this format should help increase your success rate in obtaining approvals for your proposals. To strengthen your chances even more, try following these suggestions:

1. If the proposal must be submitted by a certain deadline, make sure it reaches the client prior to that time.
2. Indicate in your letter of transmittal that the proposal is based on your current knowledge of the client's needs. State that if those needs are different or have changed, you are willing and able to modify the proposal accordingly.
3. If you haven't received an answer after a reasonable

period of time (usually one to three weeks), don't be afraid to contact the client to verify the status of your proposal. At this time you might also offer to answer any questions that the client may have concerning the proposal.

4. Don't push too hard, trying to force the client to give you an early answer. This pressure may result in an answer, but probably not the one you want.

THE CONSULTING CONTRACT

The issue of whether or not to use a contract can be a touchy one. On the plus side, a contract spells out the terms of your agreement with the client, helps to avert misunderstandings from occurring, and, if necessary, can be used as evidence in a court of law. On the minus side, clients are often put off by contracts, particularly lengthy ones packed with legal phrases. In this instance, instead of facilitating your agreement, the contract distances you from the client. What's more, since the services of an attorney are usually needed to draw up a contract correctly, additional time and expense are required.

What should you do then—use a contract or not use a contract? The majority of consultants we spoke to use a variation of the formal contract, or what's known as a "letter of agreement." We have found that this almost always meets our purposes too. Unlike the document an attorney prepares, a letter of agreement is written in plain language on your stationery and usually isn't more than three pages long. Essentially, it's nothing more than a detailed proposal with spaces for you and the client to sign the agreement, thereby accepting its terms.

What to Put in Your Letters of Agreement

Your letters of agreement should provide at least the following information:

1. *The names of the parties involved.* In order to be valid, the agreement must specify what persons are to be bound by its terms.

2. *The consulting services to be performed.* The information provided in the "summary" and "scope of the work" sections of your proposal goes here, along with any other details that are relevant to the assignment. Be as specific as you can and, whenever possible, quantify the tasks you will perform. For example, writing "Consultant will conduct focus group interviews for the client" is too vague. Who will the consultant interview? How many sessions will there be? "Consultant will interview thirty women between the ages of eighteen and forty-five in two three-hour focus group sessions" provides the missing details.

3. *Start and stop dates.* When will you start work on the assignment and how long will it take you to complete it? Without this information, your agreement is worthless, since there must be some stipulation as to the time frame when the services will be provided. Stating that "interviews are to be conducted during the month of March" solves the problem.

4. *Fees and payment schedule.* A contract is only binding when both parties give something of value to each other. Thus, you must indicate what you are to receive in exchange for your services, clarifying the fee arrangement you and the client have agreed upon and the payment schedule that is to be used. For example: "Consultant is to receive $2,000, 50 percent due prior to starting the assignment and 50 percent due within thirty days after the assignment is completed."

5. *Expenses.* Are client-related expenses to be billed to the client, or are they included in your overall fee? This obviously has a bearing on the amount of your fee and the type of fee arrangement you use. *Never assume* that you will be reimbursed for expenses you incur on the client's behalf. This should be discussed ahead of time and written into your letter of agreement.

6. *Support services the client is to provide.* The support services, if any, that the client will provide should also be listed in your agreement. They include such things as office space, secretarial assistance, telephone service, and photocopying.

In most instances, this information should be sufficient to protect your rights and the client's. However, for additional protection, you may want to clarify such points as:

Your employment status. For tax and insurance purposes, it's advisable to indicate that you are an independent contractor and not an employee. As such, you have neither the rights nor the obligations of an employee.

The use of subcontractors. Make it clear whether or not you have the right to subcontract part of the work on the assignment to outside persons or firms. In the event that this is permitted, the client may wish to retain the right of final approval over anyone you hire.

Confidentiality. Many consulting contracts contain a clause stating that any information the client reveals to the consultant will be kept confidential. This assures clients that their privacy will be maintained and that others won't have access to their information.

Attorney's fees. This stipulates who will be responsible for the payment of attorney's fees should it be necessary to use an attorney to resolve any legal disputes that may arise. Usually it's stated that all court and attorney's fees shall be paid by the party who does not prevail in the lawsuit.

Your letters of agreement can address other issues besides the ones described. In fact, there are probably as many different types of letters of agreement as there are different types of consultants. If you are uncertain what to include in your agreements or the correct wording to use, *do* contact an attorney. For more information specifically related to government contracts, see Chapter 10.

REPORTS AND RECOMMENDATIONS

Reports provide a means of communicating with clients and documenting your consulting activities. During a consulting project, *progress reports* enable the client to follow your progress and stay actively involved in what you are working to accomplish. Once a project has been completed, a well-written *summary report* can assist the client in implementing your recommendations.

Report Guidelines

The following guidelines will help you to get the most mileage out of the reports you prepare for clients.

Progress reports should:

- Be timely. The main purpose of progress reports is to inform the client of the developments that are occurring throughout the consulting assignment. To achieve this end, your progress reports should coincide with the various stages of the assignment.
- Be succinct and to the point. Verbose, rambling reports not only take longer to prepare but are generally disdained by clients. If you really want to win over clients, show your respect for their time by sticking to the facts.
- Highlight your findings and/or accomplishments. The discoveries you have made, the tasks you have completed—these are the meat of your progress reports. As such, they should be chronicled in an accurate and thorough manner, thus enabling the client to derive the full value from your efforts.
- Detail any problems you have encountered. The client has a right to be informed of any problems you encounter in performing your consulting services since these may affect the client. In reporting problems, try to be as objective as possible, neither minimizing the importance of a problem nor blowing it out of proportion.
- Estimate the percentage of the work you have completed. Estimating the work you have completed helps to reassure the client that progress *is* being made. This estimate is particularly important on long-term projects which, from the client's point of view, often can seem to stretch out into infinity.
- Explain what you intend to do next. Rather than leaving the client in the dark, outline the steps you plan to take in the next phase of the assignment. Providing prior notice in

this way increases the client's involvement in the project and enables you to affirm that your proposed actions are in keeping with the client's wishes.

- Offer your recommendations to date. Depending on the consulting assignment, it may be in the client's best interests to submit your recommendations at periodic intervals throughout the assignment instead of waiting until after your work is completed. If so, these recommendations should be included in your progress reports.

Summary reports should:

- Provide an overview of the assignment. This sets forth the circumstances surrounding the consulting assignment and states its objectives.
- Document the activities that took place. What did you do and why? Your summary report should detail the tasks that you performed on the client's behalf and the purposes they served.
- Highlight your findings and/or accomplishments. To present the whole picture, include both your current findings and those contained in any progress reports you have already submitted to the client. Try to be as specific as possible in this section, backing up your statements with the appropriate facts and figures.
- Present your recommendations. Having completed the consulting assignment, what are your recommendations? This is the most important part of your summary report since it shows the client what needs to be done to achieve the desired objectives.
- Suggest methods of implementation. Recommendations alone may not be enough for the client. Often what's needed is a step-by-step blueprint for carrying out the recommendations. This explains how and when the various actions should be taken.
- Emphasize the benefits the client is drawing from your efforts. To encourage the client to follow through on your recommendations, be sure to point out the benefits associated with this. Any benefits that the client has already received as a result of your actions should also be itemized.

8

Managing Your Time

ONE THING all consultants have in common, regardless of specialization, is the need to utilize their time effectively. Consulting is a labor-intensive business in which the primary product is time—your time. What you are able to accomplish as a consultant will largely depend on your ability to preserve this time and channel it into profitable activities. Thus, along with the other skills you process, you must also include this one: time management.

To become more proficient at time management, start by asking yourself the all-important question "How do I currently spend my time?" Even though consultants bill for their time and are more adept than most at accounting for it, time still has a way of getting out of hand. Projects that are estimated to have taken forty hours to complete turn out to have taken sixty hours or more. Part of the reason for this discrepancy is that consulting generally requires you to juggle several activities at once. Rather than sticking with a single assignment until it's finished, you're likely to be working on other projects at the same time. And then there's the consulting practice itself to run. Given this intermingling of activities, it's easy to lose track of the time.

KEEPING A TIME LOG

The simplest way to find out where your time goes is to keep a daily record, or *time log,* detailing how each working hour is

DAILY TIME LOG   **Date** _____

Consulting Activities

7:00_____   3:00_____

_____   _____

_____   _____

8:00_____   4:00_____

_____   _____

_____   _____

9:00_____   5:00_____

_____   _____

_____   _____

10:00_____   6:00_____

_____   _____

_____   _____

11:00_____   7:00_____

_____   _____

_____   _____

12:00_____   8:00_____

_____   _____

_____   _____

1:00_____   9:00_____

_____   _____

_____   _____

2:00_____   10:00_____

_____   _____

_____   _____

spent. By filling in a time log similar to the one shown here, you can accurately determine the amount of time that you spend on each separate activity.

For instance, you may be surprised to learn that a "five-minute" phone consultation with a client actually lasted twenty minutes. The "minute or so" that it takes to go over the bills each week is closer to two hours. Time frequently does not go where it's supposed to go or where you think it has gone. Everyday interruptions, unforeseen occurrences and emergencies have a way of eating into one's time. Add to this the not-uncommon tendency of consultants to set unrealistic daily goals for themselves, fully expecting to accomplish two days' work in one day's time. Such ambition and diligence is commendable but misguided. Instead of leading to higher productivity, it leads to workaholic behavior, frustration, and eventual burnout.

After a week or two of keeping a daily time log, you should ask yourself the following questions:

- How many hours did I spend on:
  Consulting projects?
  Promoting my services?
  Running my office?
  Other activities?
- How many hours did I spend on activities that I would categorize as time wasters?
- What situations happened over which I had no control?
- Which activities should receive more of my time?
- Which activities should receive less of my time?
- Did I accomplish the things I set out to do?

INCREASING YOUR QUALITY TIME

Knowing where your time goes is just the beginning. Increasing the amount of *quality time* you have to spend comes next. Quality time—when you are actively pursuing your goals creatively and constructively—can be hard to come by. To maximize the amount of quality time you have available for consulting activities, you must overcome certain obstacles. Specifically, you must reduce or eliminate as many time wasters as possible—those that you have already identified and those that you may have overlooked.

Taken individually—a minute here and a minute there—time wasters don't seem to amount to much. But when totaled, they can actually eclipse the amount of time you spend productively. Examples of time wasters include: waiting for a client who's late for an appointment, having your telephone call placed on hold, looking for a misplaced file, resubmitting a bill that was sent to the wrong person. Each one cuts into your quality time. As shown in the following list, time wasters can be internally generated by you or externally generated by other people or outside events. An inadequate filing system, which causes you to spend too much time looking for things, is an internal time waster since you can control it. However, waiting for a client to show up for an appointment is an external time waster because you have no control over it.

TIME WASTERS

Internal	External
Unorganized desk	Telephone interruptions
Inadequate filing system	Waiting for clients
Improper tools or equipment	Equipment breakdowns
Inefficient work layout	Needless meetings
Poor scheduling	Lack of information
Failure to communicate	Misinformation
Insufficient planning	Excessive paperwork
Indecision	Red tape
Lack of priorities	Incompetent people
Duplicated efforts	Misunderstandings
Spreading yourself too thin	Unclear policies and procedures
Unwillingness to delegate tasks	Hold-ups in obtaining approvals
Unclear objectives	
Inability to say no	
Procrastination	

Internally generated time wasters are the easiest to eliminate because they are the result of your own actions. Once these actions are changed, the time waster disappears. Externally generated time wasters are more of a problem. Since they are beyond your control, you can't totally eliminate them. In some instances they can be minimized, but in others you may simply need to learn how to accept them.

CONSULTANT'S TIME-MANAGEMENT SYSTEM

By employing the following strategies, you should be in a better position to overcome time wasters and increase your quality time.

Organize your work environment

Papers, files, supplies, and equipment should all be kept in their own special places, where they are out of the way but readily accessible when you need them. Equipment should be maintenanced at regular intervals. This way you won't have to waste time looking for misplaced items or waiting for crucial repairs to be made.

Set priorities

Determine in advance what goals you wish to accomplish, on both a short-term and a long-term basis, and rank them in order of importance. Then focus on those activities that must be carried out to reach the goals that have the highest priorities. Work on low-priority goals should be postponed until higher-ranking goals have been met.

Identify high-productivity hours

In allocating your time, it helps to identify those hours during the day when you are at peak efficiency. Some people work better in the morning, but others don't reach their stride until the afternoon. You may find that you have periods of peak efficiency scattered throughout the day. Whatever your pattern, you should identify these times and reserve them, whenever possible, for the high-priority items on your list. Important meetings or phone calls, planning, and creating should be scheduled for your most productive times of the day.

Communicate clearly

Misunderstandings and mistakes can be costly and time-consuming. They can frequently be avoided by taking the time to communicate clearly. Just because something seems obvious to you doesn't mean it is obvious to others. Make sure that your clients understand what you are doing each step of the way. Explain what your consulting services entail as simply and concisely as you can, keeping jargon to a minimum. And ask clients to do the same with you. If you are uncertain about what a client wants done, ask the client to restate it.

Plan meetings and phone calls

Meetings and phone calls are essential to doing business. Yet, as most consultants will tell you, they can also be among the biggest time wasters if they are not planned in advance. When making a phone call to a current or prospective client, decide what you want to say before placing the call. Write notes, if necessary, to remind yourself of the points you want to make. Before scheduling a meeting, ask yourself exactly what the meeting is to accomplish—provide a progress report, generate new business, or fulfill some other purpose? Then be prepared to discuss those topics that relate to the purpose at hand.

Set time limits

If meetings with clients are taking longer than you feel is necessary or clients keep you waiting while they attend to something else, set time limits. Let people know that the meeting must be concluded at a certain time. Psychiatrists and psychologists frequently use the "fifty-minute hour," concluding therapy sessions ten minutes before the hour is up so they have time to prepare for the next meeting. This tactic may or may not work for you. A less abrupt way of speeding things along is to tell clients that you have another appointment to keep. Billing at an hourly rate is another possibility, giving clients the option of taking up less of your time or paying you for more of it.

Learn others' policies and procedures

When your clients are businesspersons, ask them to spell out their companies' policies and procedures in advance. This will reduce misunderstandings and enable you to cut through red tape more quickly. Rather than fighting the system and creating ill will in the process, you can work within the system. Note that if you are selling your consulting services to the government, playing by the rules is critical.

Use remnant time

Remnant time—the intervals between scheduled activities—is quite often wasted. It can be the fifteen-minute gap between lunch and a meeting, the half hour wait to receive necessary information. Bit by bit the remnant time adds up. One way to have more quality time for high-priority activities is to use these odd remnants of time to take care of low-priority or routine activities. Returning a phone call, writing a personal note, catching up on your reading, or checking supplies could be accomplished during remnant time.

Learn to say no

By learning to say no, you can cut back not only on time wasters but also on the stress caused by taking on too many responsibilities. The next time you are asked to join an organization or serve on a committee, stop and ask yourself these questions: Is this something I really want to do? Would it be a good use of my time? Could someone else just as easily do it? Instead of spreading yourself too thin by trying to be involved in everything, choose the activities that are most in keeping with your goals. The same applies to consulting assignments. Difficult as it is to turn business away, if you don't think an assignment is right for you, then say no to it. Otherwise you'll end up doing the work but deriving little satisfaction from it.

Act now

Probably the biggest time waster of all is procrastination— putting off till tomorrow what can be done today. Once you've made a decision to do something or accepted an assignment, begin to lay the groundwork for carrying it out. By acting now, rather than later, you have a better chance of actually accomplishing what you set out to do. The quality of your work should be better, too, since you won't have to rush to complete it.

SETTING PRIORITIES

In setting priorities for the things you wish to accomplish, it helps to use a *daily planner* similar to the one shown on page 102. Consisting of a "things to do" list, a priority chart, and a schedule, the daily planner enables you to rank your activities in order of importance and track the progress of each task through to completion. Activities that are not completed by the end of the day are carried over to the next day, the day after that, and so on, until eventually they are either completed or eliminated.

The important thing to remember in organizing your time is that you should always give your attention to top-priority items first. Low-priority items can be tempting, especially when they are easier to do and take up less time, but it's a mistake to start with them. If you do, you may never finish the top- and high-priority tasks. So instead of completing three low-priority items, you would do better to complete 20 percent of the work on one top-priority item.

Granted, setting priorities and sticking to them isn't easy. There will always be those days when everything cries out for your immediate attention and all of your projects should have been completed yesterday. But as your time management skills improve, these days will become fewer and farther between.

DAILY PLANNER	Date _____	Schedule

THINGS TO DO

7:00

_____ _____

8:00

_____ _____

9:00

_____ _____

10:00

_____ _____

11:00

_____ _____

12:00

_____ _____

1:00

Priorities	Comments/Status	
		2:00
Top		3:00
		4:00
High		5:00
		6:00
Med.		7:00
		8:00
Low		9:00
		10:00

MEETING DEADLINES

Anyone who becomes a consultant must be prepared to meet deadlines. Much as you might want to ignore them, deadlines are an inescapable part of consulting life. Along with meetings, proposals, projects, and fees, they come with the territory. As such, it's essential that your time management system includes provisions for meeting deadlines.

To keep deadlines from getting the best of you, try following these suggestions:

1. *Give yourself enough time.* In agreeing to a deadline, don't accept one that is unrealistically short. Otherwise, you're just setting yourself up for failure.

2. *Don't have two deadlines on the same day.* It's hard enough meeting one deadline, let alone two. If doubling up is unavoidable, then move one of the dates up and plan to complete one project *ahead* of time and the other one *on* time.

3. *Establish minideadlines.* Instead of trying to meet one major deadline, establish separate "minideadlines" for completing parts of the assignment. This way you can monitor your progress and take corrective action if you start to fall behind schedule.

4. *Remember Murphy's Law.* According to Murphy, "What can go wrong will go wrong." So when planning your schedule, leave yourself a little extra time cushion in case something goes wrong and you're unable to work as quickly as anticipated.

5. *Ask for an extension, if necessary.* Your best efforts notwithstanding, if it becomes apparent that you are going to miss a deadline, ask for an extension. This should be done before the deadline is missed, and you should explain the reasons for the delay (the project has grown, you're waiting for additional information, and so on). As long as your explanation is plausible, there's a good chance the client will agree to the extension.

Using a Gantt Chart

Many consultants find that the best way to keep track of an assignment's progress is to use a Gantt chart. As shown in the following example, a Gantt chart is a pictorial representation of the work flow on a specific project. The chart enables you to see the separate activities that need to be done and the time frame for their completion. Not only does the chart show when each task should begin and end, but it also shows the various interrelationships among the tasks and the points at which they overlap.

Invented by Henry Gantt in the early 1900s, the Gantt chart was initially used to schedule jobs in factories. Since that time, though, its application has broadened considerably to the point that it is now used by managers and consultants in virtually all fields. In addition to using the Gantt chart to outline the stages of a single project, you can also use it to compare the status of separate projects and activities. This will enable you to schedule work on one project so that it coincides with the lulls in another project.

GANTT CHART

Marketing Research Project

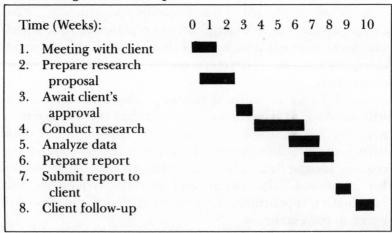

Note: The time line can be in days, weeks, or months. The number sequence can be multiples such as 0, 2, 4, 6, or 0, 4, 8, 12.

9

Using Outside Support Services

PROSPECTIVE consultants are often surprised to learn that more than 50 percent of all consulting firms are one-person operations. Even when others are employed in the business, consulting practices by their very nature tend to be small, with 25 percent of all firms ranging in size from 2 to 10 persons. As a result, in most instances owners are directly involved not only in carrying out consulting assignments but also in conducting a major portion of the activities associated with running a business. How do they do everything? By using outside support services.

There are many outside services that are willing and eager to help your consulting firm succeed. Whether you need help in obtaining financing, keeping your books in order, designing a brochure to promote your business, or simply want someone to type your letters or answer your phone, help is available.

TYPES OF SUPPORT SERVICES

Some of the individuals and institutions you can turn to for help when you need it are listed on the next page.

Accountants
Answering services
Attorneys
Bankers
Brochure specialists
Chambers of commerce
Colleges and universities
Consultants

Government agencies
Insurance agents
Libraries
Temporary-help services
Trade and professional
    associations
Word-processing services

Each of these support services can provide you with the information and assistance that otherwise might not be readily accessible to your consulting firm.

Accountants

An accountant can be instrumental in helping you to keep your consulting firm operating on a sound financial basis. Even if you are already familiar with recordkeeping procedures or employ a part-time bookkeeper to maintain your records, you may still be able to benefit from the services of an outside accountant. In addition to designing an accounting system that's suitable for your specific needs, an accountant can assist in the following tasks;

• Determining cash requirements
• Budgeting
• Forecasting
• Controlling costs
• Preparing financial statements
• Interpreting financial data
• Obtaining loans
• Preparing tax returns

You can find public accountants listed in the Yellow Pages of the telephone directory, but for the best results it's advisable to try to locate one through a personal recommendation. Another approach is to obtain the name of an accountant through one of the national or state accounting associations. Two of the larger associations are:

American Institute of Certified Public Accountants
666 Fifth Avenue
New York, NY 10019

National Society of Public Accountants
919 Eighteenth Street, N.W.
Washington, D.C. 20006

Answering Services

One of a consulting firm's strongest assets can turn out to be a good answering service. Aside from answering your phone and relaying messages, an answering service can help you to work more efficiently by screening callers or paging you when you are out of the office. And by answering your phone in a courteous and professional manner, an answering service enhances your credibility as a consultant. Unfortunately, though, not all answering services are created equal. Some seem to specialize in rudeness or have a habit of misplacing messages. Given the disparities among answering services, many consultants prefer to take matters into their own hands and use a machine to answer the phone. Either method is fine so long as it gets the job done. If you decide to use an answering service, *listen* to the various services available and compare how they respond to callers. Then choose the service that is most in keeping with the type of image you want to project.

Attorneys

An attorney can be useful in your consulting firm from the beginning, helping you to determine which legal form is best for you, preparing and filing the necessary paperwork to get started, and so on. Once your business is underway, you may need an attorney from time to time to interpret legal documents, draw up contracts, or represent you in court. The best way to find an attorney is through business acquaintances, your accountant or banker. Your state's bar association also can provide you with the names of attorneys in your area.

Bankers

Your banker can be a valuable business ally, providing a variety of financial information, advice, and services. These include helping you to prepare financial reports, obtain a line of credit, transfer funds, bill customers, and more. And since bankers come into contact with many different segments of the community, your banker may be in a position to hear news that affects your consulting firm before you do.

The time to begin establishing a good working relationship with your banker is *before* you need a loan. Start by making an appointment to meet the manager of the branch where your banking transactions will take place. The purpose of this meeting is to open a channel of communication between the two of you. Rather than just being another number on a ledger, you want to differentiate your account from the others. Providing the banker with a brief summary of your background and business objectives can add another dimension to the facts already on paper. You might also offer to keep the banker posted on the progress of your consulting firm by sending your financial reports to the bank on a regular basis.

Brochure Specialists

A brochure specialist can help you to design and produce the type of brochure that will effectively promote your consulting services. Brochure specialists know how to:

- Write and edit copy
- Create graphics
- Arrange the layout of a brochure
- Deal with printers

If yours is one of the many consulting fields in which a well-designed brochure is practically a prerequisite for obtaining new clients, you should consider using this type of support service. You can find brochure specialists by looking in the Yellow Pages under "Advertising—Direct Mail" and "Graphic Designers," or by checking with the printers in your area.

Chambers of Commerce

As a consultant, it can be to your advantage to utilize the resources of your local chamber of commerce. The traditional role of each chamber is to represent the business interests of its community and to promote the area's economy. In addition to providing you with marketing information and other data, the chamber can be a means of making business contacts and obtaining client referrals. To find out more about the various services available to you through the chamber of commerce, contact the chapter in your community.

Colleges and Universities

This is another support service that shouldn't be overlooked; educational institutions offer access to information, skills, and training through:

- Libraries, containing books, periodicals, government reports, reference works, maps, charts, audiovisual aids.
- Professors who are knowledgeable in a variety of business-related areas.
- Labor in the form of students who are receiving training in your field.
- Additional education in the form of classes in management theory, business operations, advertising methods, and other related areas.
- Seminars designed especially for small business owners (often sponsored by the Small Business Administration).

Consultants

Sometimes what a consultant needs is the services of another consultant. For example, a marketing consultant can help you to research potential markets and develop a promotional strategy for selling your services. A government relations consultant can assist you in obtaining government contracts. A data-processing consultant can improve your ability to store and retrieve information. Whatever your needs, there is likely to be a consultant who can fulfill them.

Government Agencies

Agencies of the government at the local, state, and federal levels can provide you with an abundance of useful information at little or no cost. Among those agencies whose services you might want to use are:

Department of Commerce. This department oversees the research and distribution of economic information, which is available to the public in the form of publications and reports, including:

- "Survey of Current Business," a monthly periodical that provides updates on changes in the nation's economy and the levels of business production and distribution.
- "Census Bureau Reports," covering such topics as population statistics (age, income, level of education, family status, and other demographic data); manufacturing, business, and agricultural trends.

In addition to these reports, Commerce Department specialists can advise you in such specific areas as domestic and foreign marketing opportunities, contacting foreign representatives, and deciphering tariff and trade regulations. To find the DOC office that is closest to you, check the phone directory white pages under "United States Government" or write to the Department of Commerce in Washington, D.C.

Economic Development Offices. Many communities maintain their own economic development offices, which consultants can utilize. They differ from chambers of commerce in that they are maintained by local governments rather than local businesses. They can provide you with current statistical data regarding the economy, building activity, sales trends, labor force, wages and salaries, banking, community services, and so on.

Government Printing Office. This organization oversees the publication and distribution of government documents, pamphlets, reports, and books on a variety of subjects, many of which are directly related to business. Depending on the type of consulting work you do, some of them may be of interest to you. To receive a catalog of the publications available, write to the U.S. Government Printing Office, Superintendent of Documents, Washington, D.C. 20402.

Internal Revenue Service. The IRS can answer any questions you have concerning your federal income taxes. Tax specialists in local IRS offices can handle specific questions or you can refer to any of their numerous guides and publications. One particularly valuable guide is the *Tax Guide for Small Businesses*, which is updated annually. It contains approximately two hundred pages of information covering books and records, accounting periods, determining gross profit, deductable expenses, depreciation, and other topics. This publication is available free of charge at your local IRS office. Some of the other IRS publications you can obtain are listed later on in this chapter.

Postal Service. The postal service can provide you with information to help you reduce mailing costs and use the mails more efficiently. This can be especially helpful if you plan to use direct-mail advertising as a means of reaching prospective clients. The following publications can be obtained free from your local postmaster, or by writing to the U.S. Postal Service, Washington, D.C. 20260:

- "Domestic Postage Rates and Fees"
- "How to Prepare Second- and Third-Class Mailings"
- "Mailing Permits"
- "How to Pack and Wrap Parcels for Mailing"

Small Business Administration. The SBA is designed to aid small businesses by helping them to obtain financing, providing them with management and technical assistance, conducting business seminars and workshops, and assisting in procuring government contracts (see Chapter 10).

This assistance is achieved through the operation of field offices, the distribution of publications, and the activities of the Service Corps of Retired Executives (SCORE) and the Active Corps of Executives (ACE), volunteer groups of professionals who assist the SBA in advising small businesses. A sampling of the publications produced by the SBA is shown later in the chapter, along with the addresses of the SBA field offices.

Insurance Agents

The importance of insurance and the different types of coverage available were discussed in Chapter 3. An insurance agent can analyze your consulting firm's specific needs and help you to obtain adequate coverage. Aspects of risk management that you should discuss with your agent include how to protect your assets, workers, and earnings. The best ways to find an insurance agent are through recommendations and comparison shopping. Talking to more than one agent not only lets you evaluate the levels of coverage and costs of different plans but also gives you an idea of which agent is the most knowledgeable about your type of business.

Libraries

Much of the information consultants need to operate their businesses can be obtained free of charge from libraries. It can be found not only in books but also in the assortment of magazines, newspapers, reference works, government publications, maps, charts, and audiovisual aids that are available. Technical explanations, statistical data, industry updates, trends, and economic forecasts are just some of the subject areas in which you can find information. In addition to public libraries, there are specialized libraries sponsored by colleges and universities; private industry, trade, and professional associations; labor unions and research centers.

Temporary Help Services

On those occasions when you need outside help to stay on top of the workload or complete a project, a temporary help service is the answer. It can provide well-qualified, temporary help on a moment's notice. Whether you need a typist, bookkeeper, editor, researcher, or other clerical or professional help, a temporary help service should be able to meet your personnel requirements. As an added bonus, temporary help services take care of all screening, interviewing, and testing of applicants along with the checking of references.

Trade and Professional Associations

Trade and professional associations—organizations whose members are in the same industry or perform the same services—can be particularly helpful to consultants. Both types of associations are concerned with helping their members to become more productive and cope with business problems. In many instances professional associations set the standards for their fields, formulating codes of ethics and advocating certain policies and procedures. It's not uncommon for trade and professional associations to offer assistance in such areas as accounting, promotion, public relations, and research. The majority of associations also have ongoing government relations programs, thus enabling members to have a collective voice in communicating with the government. And through their meetings and seminars, associations make it possible for individuals to come into contact with others in their fields.

To obtain information on trade and professional associations or to find out which ones represent consultants in your particular field, write to:

American Society of Association Executives
1101 Sixteenth Street, N.W.
Washington, D.C. 20036

Two other sources of information, which are available at

most public libraries, are these directories: *National Trade and Professional Associations of the United States and Canada* (Washington, D.C.: Columbia Books), and the *Encyclopedia of Associations* (Vol. 1, *National Organizations of the U.S.*: Detroit: Gale Research Co.). Both are updated periodically.

Word-Processing Services

The widespread availability of electronic typewriters and personal computers has resulted in a growing number of word-processing services. They can be invaluable to you as a consultant, helping you to produce professional-looking proposals and reports, handle correspondence, and create direct-mail materials to promote your business. In addition to general word processing, many services specialize in meeting the needs of those in the legal, medical, financial, engineering, and academic fields. To locate word-processing services in your vicinity, check the Yellow Pages under "Word Processing."

GOVERNMENT PUBLICATIONS

The following is a sampling of the publications that have been prepared by the Internal Revenue Service and the Small Business Administration.

INTERNAL REVENUE SERVICE PUBLICATIONS

Title	No.
Employer's Tax Guide, Circular E	15
Your Federal Income Tax	17
Tax Guide for Small Businesses	334
Self-Employment Tax Tables	421
Entertainment, Travel, and Gift Expenses	463
Tax Withholding and Estimated Tax	505
Self-Employment Tax	533

SMALL BUSINESS ADMINISTRATION
Free Publications

SMALL BUSINESS ADMINISTRATION
For-Sale Publications

SMALL BUSINESS ADMINISTRATION
Field Office Addresses

Alabama

908 South 20th Street
Room 202
Birmingham, AL 35205
205/254-1344

Alaska

1016 West 6th Avenue
Suite 200
Anchorage, AK 95501
907/217-4022

101 12th Avenue
Box 14
Fairbanks, AK 99701
907/452-1951

Arizona

3030 North Central Avenue
Suite 1201
Phoenix, AZ 85012
602/241-2200

301 West Congress Street
Room 3V
Tucson, AZ 85701
602/792-6715

Arkansas

320 W. Capital Ave.
Suite 601 (P.O. Box 1401)
Little Rock, AR 72201
501/378-5871

California

450 Golden Gate Avenue
P.O. Box 36044
San Francisco, CA 94102
415/556-7487

211 Main Street
4th Floor
San Francisco, CA 94105
415/556-7490

1515 Clay Street
Oakland, CA 94612
415/273-7790

1229 "N" Street
Fresno, CA 93712
209/487-5189

2800 Cottage Way
Room W2535
Sacramento, CA 95825
916/484-4726

350 S. Figueroa Street
6th Floor
Los Angeles, CA 90071
213/688-2956

880 Front Street
Room 4-S-33
San Diego, CA 92188
714/293-5440

2700 North Main Street
Suite 400
Santa Ana, CA 92701
714/836-2494

Colorado

Executive Tower Building
1405 Curtis Street
22nd Floor
Denver, CO 80202
303/837-5763

721 19th Street
Room 407
Denver, CO 80202
303/837-2607

Connecticut

One Financial Plaza
Hartford, CT 06103
203/244-3600

Delaware

844 King Street
Room 5207
Lockbox 16
Wilmington, DE 19801
302/573-6294

District of Columbia

1030 15th Street, N.W.
Suite 250
Washington, D.C. 20417
202/653-6965

Florida

400 West Bay Street
Room 261
P.O. Box 35067
Jacksonville, FL 32202
904/791-3782

2222 Ponce De Leon Boulevard
5th Floor
Coral Gables, FL 33134
305/350-5521

700 Twiggs Street
Suite 607
Tampa, FL 33602
813/228-2594

701 Clematis Street
Room 229
West Palm Beach, FL 33402
305/659-7533

Georgia

1375 Peachtree Street, N.W.
5th Floor
Atlanta, GA 30309
404/881-4943

1720 Peachtree Road, N.W.
6th Floor
Atlanta, GA 30309
404/881-4325

Federal Building
52 North Main Street
Statesboro, GA 30458
912/489-8719

Guam

Pacific Daily News Building
Room 508
Martyr and Chara Sts.
Agana, Guam 96910
671/477-8420

Hawaii

300 Ala Moana
Room 2213
P.O. Box 50207
Honolulu, HI 96850
808/546-8950

Idaho

1005 Main Street
2nd Floor
Boise, ID 83702
208/334-1096

Illinois

219 South Dearborn Street
Room 838
Chicago, IL 60604
312/353-4528

219 South Dearborn Street
Room 438
Chicago, IL 60604
312/353-4528

1 North Old State Capital Plaza
Springfield, IL 62701
217/525-4416

Indiana

575 North Pennsylvania Street
Room 552
Indianapolis, IN 46204
317/269-7272

Iowa

210 Walnut Street
Room 749
Des Moines, IA 50309
515/284-4422

373 Collins Road, N.E.
Cedar Rapids, IA 52402
319/366-2411

Kansas

Main Place Bldg.
110 East Waterman Street
Wichita, KS 67202
316/267-6311

Kentucky
600 Federal Place
Room 188
Louisville, KY 40201
502/582-5971

Louisiana
1001 Howard Avenue
17th Floor
New Orleans, LA 70113
504/589-6685

500 Fannin Street
Room 5 B04
Shreveport, LA 71101
318/226-5196

Maine
40 Western Avenue
Room 512
Augusta, ME 04330
207/622-6171

Maryland
8600 LaSalle Road
Room 630
Towson, MD 21204
301/962-4392

Massachusetts
60 Batterymarch Street
10th Floor
Boston, MA 02110
617/223-2100

150 Causeway Street
10th Floor
Boston, MA 02114
617/223-2100

302 High Street
4th Floor
Holyoke, MA 01040
413/536-8770

Michigan
477 Michigan Avenue
Room 515
Detroit, MI 48226
313/226-6000

Don H. Bottum University Ctr.
540 W. Kaye Avenue
Marquette, MI 49885
906/225-1108

Minnesota
Plymouth Bldg.
Room 530
12 South 6th Street
Minneapolis, MN 55402
612/725-2362

Mississippi
100 West Capitol Street
Suite 322
Jackson, MS 39201
601/969-4371

111 Fred Haise Boulevard
2nd Floor
Biloxi, MS 39530
601/435-3676

Missouri
911 Walnut Street
23rd Floor
Kansas City, MO 64106
816/374-5288

1150 Grand Avenue
5th Floor
Kansas City, MO 64106
816/374-3416

One Mercantile Tower
Suite 2500
St. Louis, MO 63101
314/425-4191

731 North Main
Sikeston, MO 63801
314/471-0223

Montana
301 South Park Avenue
Room 528, Drawer 10054
Helena, MT 59601
406/449-5381

Nebraska

19th & Farnum Streets
2nd Floor
Omaha, NE 68102
402/221-4691

Nevada

301 E. Stewart
P.O. Box 7527
Downtown Station
Las Vegas, NV 89101
702/385-6611

50 South Virginia Street
Room 308
P.O. Box 3216
Reno, NV 89505
702/784-5268

New Hampshire

55 Pleasant Street
Room 211
Concord, NH 03301
603/224-4041

New Jersey

970 Broad Street
Room 1635
Newark, NJ 07102
201/645-2434

1800 East Davis Street
Camden, NJ 08104
609/757-5183

New Mexico

5000 Marble Avenue, N.E.
Room 320
Albuquerque, NM 87110
505/766-3430

New York

26 Federal Plaza
Room 29-118
New York, NY 10007
212/264-7772

26 Federal Plaza
Room 3100
New York, NY 10007
212/264-4355

401 Broad Hollow Road
Suite 322
Melville, NY 11747
516/752-1626

100 South Clinton Street
Room 1073
Syracuse, NY 13260
315/423-5383

111 West Huron Street
Room 1311
Buffalo, NY 14202
716/846-4301

180 State Street
Room 412
Elmira, NY 14901
607/734-4686

99 Washington Avenue
Room 921
Albany, NY 12210
518/472-6300

100 State Street
Room 601
Rochester, NY 14614
716/263-6700

North Carolina

230 S. Tryon Street
Suite 700
Charlotte, NC 28202
704/371-6111

215 South Evans Street
Room 206
Greenville, NC 27834
919/752-3798

North Dakota

653 2nd Avenue, North
Room 218
P.O. Box 3086
Fargo, ND 58102
701/237-5771

Ohio

1240 East 9th Street
Room 317
Cleveland, OH 44199
216/522-4180

85 Marconi Boulevard
Columbus, OH 43215
614/469-6860

550 Main Street
Room 5028
Cincinnati, OH 45202
513/684-2814

Oklahoma

200 N.W. 5th Street
Suite 670
Oklahoma City, OK 73102
405/231-4301

333 W. Fourth Street
Room 3104
Tulsa, OK 74103
918/581-7462

Oregon

1220 S.W. Third Avenue
Room 676
Portland, OR 97204
503/221-2682

Pennsylvania

One Bala Cynwyd Plaza
231 St. Asaphs Rd.
Suite 640
West Lobby
Bala Cynwyd, PA 19004
215/596-3311

One Bala Cynwyd Plaza
231 St. Asaphs Rd.
Suite 400
East Lobby
Bala Cynwyd, PA 19004
215/596-3311

100 Chestnut Street
Room 309
Harrisburg, PA 17101
717/782-3840

Penn Place
20 N. Pennsylvania Avenue
Wilkes-Barre, PA 18702
717/826-6497

1000 Liberty Avenue
Room 1401
Pittsburgh, PA 15222
412/644-2780

Puerto Rico

Federal Building
Room 6991
Carlos Chardon Avenue
Hato Rey, PR 00919
809/753-4572

Rhode Island

40 Fountain Street
Providence, RI 02903
401/528-4586

South Carolina

1835 Assembly Street
3rd Floor
P.O. Box 2786
Columbia, SC 29201
803/765-5376

South Dakota

101 South Main Avenue
Suite 101
Sioux Falls, SD 57102
605/336-2980

515 9th Street
Room 246
Rapid City, SD 57701
605/343-5074

Tennessee

404 James Robertson Parkway
Suite 1012
Nashville, TN 37219
615/251-5881

502 South Gay Street
Room 307
Knoxville, TN 37902
615/637-9300

211 Federal Office Bldg.
167 North Main Street
Memphis, TN 38103
901/521-3588

Texas

1720 Regal Row
Room 230
Dallas, TX 75235
214/767-7643

1100 Commerce Street
Room 3C36
Dallas, TX 75242
214/767-0605

100 South Washington Street
Room G-12
Marshall, TX 75670
214/935-5257

One Allen Center
Suite 705
500 Dallas Street
Houston, TX 77002
713/660-4000

1205 Texas Avenue
Room 712
Lubbock, TX 79401
806/762-7466

4100 Rio Bravo Street
Suite 300
El Paso, TX 79902
915/543-7586

222 East Van Buren Street
Suite 500
Harlingen, TX 78550
512/423-8934

3105 Leopard Street
P.O. Box 9253
Corpus Christi, TX 78408
512/888-3331

727 East Durango Street
Room A-513
San Antonio, TX 78206
512/229-6250

300 East 8th Street
Austin, TX 78701
512/397-5288

Utah

125 South State Street
Room 2237
Salt Lake City, UT 84138
801/524-5800

Vermont

87 State Street
Room 204
Montpelier, VT 05602
802/229-0538

Virginia

400 North 8th Street
Room 3015
P.O. Box 10126
Richmond, VA 23240
804/771-2617

Virgin Islands

Veterans Drive
Room 283
St. Thomas, VI 00801
809/774-8530

Washington

710 2nd Avenue
5th Floor
Seattle, WA 98104
206/442-5676

915 Second Avenue
Room 1744
Seattle, WA 98174
206/442-5534

651 U.S. Courthouse
P.O. Box 2167
Spokane, WA 99210
509/456-5310

West Virginia

109 North 3rd Street
Room 301
Clarksburg, WV 26301
304/623-5631

Charleston National Plaza
Suite 628
Charleston, WV 25301
304/343-6181

Wisconsin

212 East Washington Avenue
Room 213
Madison, WI 53703
608/264-5261

517 East Wisconsin Avenue
Room 246
Milwaukee, WI 53202
414/291-3941

500 South Barstow Street
Room 89AA
Eau Claire, WI 54701
715/834-9012

Wyoming

100 East B Street
Room 4001
P.O. Box 2839
Casper, WY 82601
307/265-5550

10

Selling to the Government

THE United States Government is the nation's largest customer. In any given year purchases made by federal, state, and local branches of the government total between 25 and 35 percent of the gross national product. As pointed out in Chapter 1, among the many things that the government buys are consulting services. Often the government does not have the internal resources (time, personnel, expertise, and so on) to achieve its goals. Therefore, if it is to accomplish certain projects, it must often rely on outside consultations to perform the necessary tasks.

HOW THE GOVERNMENT OPERATES

While there are similarities between doing business in the private sector and doing business with the government, there are also distinct differences. For one thing, the government has predetermined purchasing procedures that must be followed. And whereas private businesses are generally free to buy from anyone they choose, the government is required to consider all qualified service providers. Not surprisingly, selling to the government also involves a lot more paperwork than selling to private businesses.

Deciphering the government's abbreviations; figuring out which person, department, or agency to contact; and complying with the required procedures isn't an easy feat. But for those consultants who are willing to take the time to learn the system, the rewards can be considerable.

Contracting Procedures

Before awarding a contract, the government usually follows one of two procedures. It issues an Invitation for Bids (IFB) or a Request for Proposals (RFP).

An *Invitation for Bids* states the needs of the procuring agency and defines the work to be done in sufficient detail to permit all bidders to respond to the invitation. Prospective bidders are provided standard forms (see example) on which to submit their bids, and a specific time for opening the bids is established. If you wish to respond to the IFB, you must submit your sealed bid prior to the bid opening time and must meet the essential requirements of the IFB. Bids that fail to do either of these are considered to be "nonresponsive" and are automatically rejected.

The bid opening is held in public and the contract is awarded to the qualified bidder whose bid is the "most advantageous to the government." In other words, *the low bidder gets the contract.* The actual award is usually made within two or three months after the bid opening. This gives the contracting officer time to check all the bids for mistakes and to make sure that the winner is in full compliance with the IFB.

A *Request for Proposals* differs from an Invitation for Bids in that it is less specific regarding the methods that the contractor must employ to carry out the assignment. Although the contracting agency has an idea of the end result that it wants to achieve and the time frame for accomplishing that result, it does not have a plan of action to follow. The purpose of the RFP is to gather as many proposals as possible so that the various approaches to carrying out the assignment can be compared. In addition to evaluating each proposal on the basis of its approach, the contracting officer or

Standard Form 33: Solicitation, Offer, and Award.

| STANDARD FORM 33, NOV. 1969 GENERAL SERVICES ADMINISTRATION FED. PROC. REG. (41 CPR) 1-16 101 | SOLICITATION, OFFER, AND AWARD | 3. CERTIFIED FOR NATIONAL DEFENSE UNDER BDSA REG. 2 AND/OR DMS REG. 1. RATING | 4. PAGE OF 1 |

| 1. CONTRACT (Proc. Inst. Ident.) NO | 2. SOLICITATION NO. ☐ ADVERTISED (IFB) ☐ NEGOTIATED (RFP) | 5. DATE ISSUED | 6. REQUISITION/PURCHASE REQUEST NO. |

| 7. ISSUED BY   CODE | 8. ADDRESS OFFER TO (If other than Block 7) |

SOLICITATION

9. Sealed offers in original and ____ copies for furnishing the supplies or services described in the Schedule will be received at the place specified in block 8, OR IF HAND-CARRIED, IN THE DEPOSITARY LOCATED IN _____ until _____ (Time, Zone, and Date) . If this is an advertised solicitation, offers will be publicly opened at that time. CAUTION—LATE OFFERS. See par. 8 of Solicitation Instructions and Conditions.

All offers are subject to the following:
1. The attached Solicitation Instructions and Conditions, SF 33-A.
2. The General Provisions, SF 32____edition, which is attached or incorporated herein by reference.
3. The Schedule included below and/or attached hereto.
4. Such other provisions, representations, certifications, and specifications as are attached or incorporated herein by reference. (Attachments are listed in the Schedule.)

FOR INFORMATION CALL (Name and Telephone No.) (No collect calls.):

SCHEDULE

10 ITEM NO.	11. SUPPLIES/SERVICES	12 QUANTITY	13. UNIT	14. UNIT PRICE	15. AMOUNT

OFFER (NOTE: Reverse Must Also Be Fully Completed By Offeror)

In compliance with the above, the undersigned offers and agrees, if this offer is accepted within____ calendar days (60 calendar days unless a different period is inserted by the offeror) from the date for receipt of offers specified above, to furnish any or all items upon which prices are offered, at the price set opposite each item, delivered at the designated point(s), within the time specified in the Schedule.

16. DISCOUNT FOR PROMPT PAYMENT (See Par. 9 on SF 33-A)
____% 10 CALENDAR DAYS; ____% 20 CALENDAR DAYS; ____% 30 CALENDAR DAYS; ____% ____ CALENDAR DAYS.

| 17. OFFEROR NAME & ADDRESS   CODE   FACILITY CODE | 18. NAME AND TITLE OF PERSON AUTHORIZED TO SIGN OFFER (Type or Print) |
| (Street, city, county, state, & ZIP Code) Area Code and Telephone No.: ☐ Check If Remittance Address Is Different From Above -Enter Such Address In Schedule. | 19. SIGNATURE | 20. OFFER DATE |

AWARD (To Be Completed By Government)

21. ACCEPTED AS TO ITEMS NUMBERED	22. AMOUNT	23. ACCOUNTING AND APPROPRIATION DATA
24. SUBMIT INVOICES (4 copies unless otherwise specified) TO ADDRESS SHOWN IN BLOCK ____	25. NEGOTIATED PURSUANT TO ☐ 10 U.S.C. 2304(a)( ) ☐ 41 U.S.C. 252(c)( )
26. ADMINISTERED BY (If other than block 7) CODE	27. PAYMENT WILL BE MADE BY CODE
28. NAME OF CONTRACTING OFFICER (Type or Print)	29. UNITED STATES OF AMERICA BY: _____ (Signature of Contracting Officer)	30. AWARD DATE

REPRESENTATIONS, CERTIFICATIONS, AND ACKNOWLEDGMENTS

The Offeror represents and certifies as part of his offer that: *(Check or complete all applicable boxes or blocks.)*

1. SMALL BUSINESS *(See par. 14 on SF 33–A.)*
He ☐ is, ☐ is not, a small business concern. If offeror is a small business concern and is not the manufacturer of the supplies offered, he also represents that all supplies to be furnished hereunder ☐ will, ☐ will not, be manufactured or produced by a small business concern in the United States, its possessions, or Puerto Rico.

2. REGULAR DEALER—MANUFACTURER *(Applicable only to supply contracts exceeding $10,000.)*
He is a ☐ regular dealer in, ☐ manufacturer of, the supplies offered.

3. CONTINGENT FEE *(See par. 15 on SF 33–A.)*
(a) He ☐ has, ☐ has not, employed or retained any company or person *(other than a full-time, bona fide employee working solely for the offeror)* to solicit or secure this contract, and (b) he ☐ has, ☐ has not, paid or agreed to pay any company or person *(other than a full-time bona fide employee working solely for the offeror)* any fee, commission, percentage, or brokerage fee contingent upon or resulting from the award of this contract; and agrees to furnish information relating to (a) and (b) above, as requested by the Contracting Officer. *(For interpretation of the representation, including the term "bona fide employee," see Code of Federal Regulations, Title 41, Subpart 1-1.5.)*

4. TYPE OF BUSINESS ORGANIZATION
He operates as ☐ an individual, ☐ a partnership, ☐ a nonprofit organization, ☐ a corporation, incorporated under the laws of the State of

5. AFFILIATION AND IDENTIFYING DATA *(Applicable only to advertised solicitations.)*
Each offeror shall complete (a) and (b) if applicable, and (c) below:
(a) He ☐ is, ☐ is not, owned or controlled by a parent company. *(See par. 16 on SF 33–A.)*
(b) If the offeror is owned or controlled by a parent company, he shall enter in the blocks below the name and main office address of the parent company:

Name of Parent company and main office address _____

(include ZIP Code)_____

(c) Employer's identification number *(See par. 17 on SF 33–A.)*_____

            (Offeror's E.I. No.)   *(Parent Company's E.I. No.)*

6. EQUAL OPPORTUNITY
He ☐ has, ☐ has not, participated in a previous contract or subcontract subject either to the Equal Opportunity clause herein or the clause originally contained in section 301 of Executive Order No. 10925, or the clause contained in section 201 of Executive Order No. 11114; that he ☐ has, ☐ has not, filed all required compliance reports; and that representations indicating submission of required compliance reports, signed by proposed subcontractors, will be obtained prior to subcontract awards. *(The above representation need not be submitted in connection with contracts or subcontracts which are exempt from the clause.)*

7. BUY AMERICAN CERTIFICATE
The offeror hereby certifies that each end product, except the end products listed below, is a domestic source end product (as defined in the *clause* entitled "Buy American Act"); and that components of unknown origin have been considered to have been mined, produced, or manufactured outside the United States.

EXCLUDED END PRODUCTS	COUNTRY OF ORIGIN

8. CERTIFICATION OF INDEPENDENT PRICE DETERMINATION *(See par. 18 on SF 33–A.)*
(a) By submission of this offer, the offeror certifies, and in the case of a joint offer, each party thereto certifies as to its own organization, that in connection with this procurement:
(1) The prices in this offer have been arrived at independently, without consultation, communication, or agreement, for the purpose of restricting competition, as to any matter relating to such prices with any other offeror or with any competitor;
(2) Unless otherwise required by law, the prices which have been quoted in this offer have not been knowingly disclosed by the offeror and will not knowingly be disclosed by the offeror prior to opening in the case of an advertised procurement or prior to award in the case of a negotiated procurement, directly or indirectly to any other offeror or to any competitor; and
(3) No attempt has been made or will be made by the offeror to induce any other person or firm to submit or not to submit an offer for the purpose of restricting competition.
(b) Each person signing this offer certifies that:
(1) He is the person in the offeror's organization responsible within that organization for the decision as to the prices being offered herein and that he has not participated, and will not participate, in any action contrary to (a) (1) through (a) (3) above; or
(2) (i) He is not the person in the offeror's organization responsible within that organization for the decision as to the prices being offered herein but that he has been authorized in writing to act as agent for the persons responsible for such decision in certifying that such persons have not participated, and will not participate, in any action contrary to (a) (1) through (a) (3) above, and as their agent does hereby so certify; and (ii) he has not participated, and will not participate, in any action contrary to (a) (1) through (a) (3) above.

9. CERTIFICATION OF NONSEGREGATED FACILITIES
(Applicable to (1) contracts, (2) subcontracts, and (3) agreements with applicants who are themselves performing federally assisted construction contracts, exceeding $10,000 which are not exempt from the provisions of the Equal Opportunity clause.)
By the submission of this bid, the bidder, offeror, applicant, or subcontractor certifies that he does not maintain or provide for his employees any segregated facilities at any of his establishments, and that he does not permit his employees to perform their services at any location, under his control, where segregated facilities are maintained. He certifies further that he will not maintain or provide for his employees any segregated facilities at any of his establishments, and that he will not permit his employees to perform their services at any location, under his control, where segregated facilities are maintained. The bidder, offeror, applicant, or subcontractor agrees that a breach of this certification is a violation of the Equal Opportunity clause in this contract. As used in this certification, the term "segregated facilities" means any waiting rooms, work areas, rest rooms and wash rooms, restaurants and other eating areas, time clocks, locker rooms and other storage or dressing areas, parking lots, drinking fountains, recreation or entertainment areas, transportation, and housing facilities provided for employees which are segregated by explicit directive or are in fact segregated on the basis of race, color, religion or national origin, because of habit, local custom, or otherwise. He further agrees that (except where he has obtained identical certifications from proposed subcontractors for specific time periods) he will obtain identical certifications from proposed subcontractors prior to the award of subcontracts exceeding $10,000 which are not exempt from the provisions of the Equal Opportunity clause; that he will retain such certifications in his files; and that he will forward the following notice to such proposed subcontractors (except where the proposed subcontractors have submitted identical certifications for specific time periods):
Notice to prospective subcontractors of requirement for certifications of nonsegregated facilities.
A Certification of Nonsegregated Facilities must be submitted prior to the award of a subcontract exceeding $10,000 which is not exempt from the provisions of the Equal Opportunity clause. The certification may be submitted either for each subcontract or for all subcontracts during a period (i.e., quarterly, semiannually, or annually). NOTE: *The penalty for making false statements in offers is prescribed in 18 U.S.C. 1001.*

ACKNOWLEDGMENT OF AMENDMENTS	AMENDMENT NO.	DATE	AMENDMENT NO.	DATE
The offeror acknowledges receipt of amendments to the Solicitation for Offers and related documents numbered and dated as follows:				

NOTE.—*Offers must set forth full, accurate, and complete information as required by this Solicitation (including attachments). The penalty for making false statements in offers is prescribed in 18 U.S.C. 1001.*

selection committee takes into consideration the proposer's experience, past performance, personnel, and other resources. Price is still a factor in awarding the contract, but, unlike the award of an IFB, being the low bidder is no guarantee that your proposal will be the one selected. Once the evaluation process has been completed, the contract is awarded to the proposer whose offer is considered to be the best.

RFP submissions (which often require the same form as an IFB) are not opened publicly, but they still must be received by the established deadline. In some instances the winning proposal is selected without any discussion with the proposer. When this happens, a Notice of Award is sent to that proposer, creating a binding contract. In other instances, discussions or negotiations are necessary before a contract can be awarded. When more than one proposal stands a chance of being selected, all competing proposers must be included in the discussions. These discussions may not disclose any information about a competitor's proposal or price. However, they may indicate any deficiencies in a proposal or if its price is too high. At the conclusion of discussions, all proposers are notified in writing of a date for submission of their final offers. The winning proposal is then selected from those received.

TYPES OF GOVERNMENT CONTRACTS

Government contracts fall into two broad categories: fixed-price contracts and cost-reimbursement contracts. The big difference between the two is that fixed-price contracts require you to perform the agreed upon work at the price that has been set—regardless of what it costs you. Under a cost-reimbursement contract you are entitled to be reimbursed for your "allowable" costs and to receive a predetermined fee (profit) for your services.

Fixed-Price Contract

Fixed-price contracts come in several shapes and sizes, including the following variations:

Firm Fixed-Price

This is the most commonly issued type of fixed-price contract. The price is firm for the duration of the contract and is not subject to any adjustments, except for authorized changes. It works best in those situations when your costs are reasonably predictable and you can arrive at a price with a high degree of accuracy. A firm fixed-price contract places maximum risk on you, the contractor, since all costs above the set price are your responsibility. On the positive side, though, if your costs are less than anticipated, your profit will be higher.

Economic Price Adjustment

Some fixed-price contracts contain economic price adjustment clauses that protect you and the government against wide fluctuations in labor or materials cost when market conditions are unstable. These clauses stipulate that the contract price can be increased (or decreased) in response to higher (or lower) costs. Frequently the contract will contain a ceiling price that the government will not exceed, no matter what the cost fluctuations may be.

Fixed-Price Redetermination

Under this type of contract, you and the government contracting officer establish an initial price for your services, a ceiling price, and a time for redetermination. At the time of redetermination, you submit a proposal based on your actual costs to date and the estimated cost of any incomplete work. After a government audit, you negotiate a revised price. This price may be higher or lower than the initial price, but it may not exceed the ceiling price.

Fixed-Price Incentive

This type of contract is similar to a redetermination contract. The difference is that an incentive contract contains a target cost and a formula for determining your profit. The formula rewards you with more profit if your actual costs are less than the target cost and takes away profit if your costs exceed the target. As with the redetermination contract, though, you cannot be paid more than the ceiling price.

Cost-Reimbursement Contracts

The following types of cost-reimbursement contracts represent those most frequently issued by the government.

Cost-Plus-Fixed-Fee

This type of contract is issued more often than any of the others in its group. Under it, you and the contracting agency agree on the estimated cost of contract performance and a fixed fee (profit) that you will receive for doing the work. In this instance, you are entitled to recover all of your allowable costs (as defined in the contract) and your fixed fee. Regardless of whether your actual costs are greater or lesser than the estimated cost, you still receive the same fee.

Cost-Plus-Incentive-Fee

The cost-plus-incentive-fee contract calls for you and the contracting officer to agree on a target cost, a target fee, and an incentive formula for determining your final fee. The formula provides for an adjustment in the fee based on any difference between the target cost and the actual cost. If your costs turn out to be less than the target cost, your fee is increased accordingly. Unlike the fixed-price-incentive contract discussed earlier, this contract doesn't have a price ceiling. However, it does place a minimum and maximum limit on the fee adjustment that can be made.

Cost-Plus-Award-Fee

In addition to reimbursing you for your costs, this contract provides for the payment of *two* kinds of fees—a base fee and an award fee. The base fee is set in advance, but the award fee is pegged to the contract officer's evaluation of your performance. Those performance areas that are rated include the quality of the work, your timeliness in completing the assignment, ingenuity shown, and cost effectiveness.

FINDING OUT ABOUT CONTRACT OFFERINGS

Before you can compete for a government contract, first you must be aware of the contract offering. The following information sources can all be utilized to find out about consulting opportunities with the government.

Bidder's Mailing Lists

One of the best ways to find out about government contracts is to be included on the Bidder's Mailing List (BML) for each government department or agency with whom you wish to do business. This can be accomplished by filling out a "Bidder's Mailing List Application," Standard Form 129, and submitting it to the appropriate procurement offices. Copies of the form, which is shown here, can be obtained from the General Services Administration, described later in the chapter, or directly from the government procurement offices.

Once your name has been placed on a Bidder's Mailing List, Invitation for Bids and Request for Proposals solicitations will automatically be sent to you. In order to remain on the list, however, you must respond to each IFB or RFP by (1) submitting a bid or proposal, or (2) writing that you are unable to bid on the transaction but wish to remain on the active Bidder's Mailing List. Failure to do either of these may result in having your name removed from the list.

BIDDER'S MAILING LIST APPLICATION	INITIAL APPLICATION	FORM APPROVED OMB NO.
	REVISION	29–R0069

Fill in all spaces. Insert "NA" in blocks not applicable. Type or print all entries. See reverse for instructions.

TO (*Enter name and address of Federal agency to which form is submitted. Include ZIP Code*) | DATE

1. APPLICANT'S NAME AND ADDRESS (*Include county and ZIP Code*) | 2. ADDRESS (*Include county and ZIP Code*) TO WHICH SOLICITATIONS ARE TO BE MAILED (*If different from item 1*)

3. TYPE OF ORGANIZATION (*Check one*)

INDIVIDUAL		PARTNERSHIP	NON-PROFIT ORGANIZATION	**4.** HOW LONG IN PRESENT BUSINESS
CORPORATION, INCORPORATED UNDER THE LAWS OF THE STATE OF				

5. NAMES OF OFFICERS, OWNERS, OR PARTNERS

PRESIDENT	VICE PRESIDENT	SECRETARY
TREASURER	OWNERS OR PARTNERS	

6. AFFILIATES OF APPLICANT (*Names, locations and nature of affiliation. See definition on reverse*)

7. PERSONS AUTHORIZED TO SIGN BIDS, OFFERS, AND CONTRACTS IN YOUR NAME (*Indicate if agent*)

NAME	OFFICIAL CAPACITY	TEL. NO. (*Incl. area code*)

8. IDENTIFY EQUIPMENT, SUPPLIES, MATERIALS, AND/OR SERVICES ON WHICH YOU DESIRE TO BID (*See attached Federal agency's supplemental listing and instructions, if any*)

9. TYPE OF OWNERSHIP (*See definitions on reverse*)

MINORITY BUSINESS ENTERPRISE	OTHER THAN MINORITY BUSINESS ENTERPRISE

10. TYPE OF BUSINESS (*See definitions on reverse*)

MANUFACTURER OR PRODUCER	REGULAR DEALER (*Type 1*)	REGULAR DEALER (*Type 2*)
SERVICE ESTABLISHMENT	CONSTRUCTION CONCERN	RESEARCH AND DEVELOPMENT FIRM

☐ SURPLUS DEALER (*Check this box if you are also a dealer in surplus goods*)

11. SIZE OF BUSINESS (*See definitions on reverse*)

SMALL BUSINESS CONCERN*	OTHER THAN SMALL BUSINESS CONCERN	
*If you are a small business concern, fill in (a) and (b):	(a) AVERAGE NUMBER OF EMPLOYEES (*Including affiliates*) FOR FOUR PRECEDING CALENDAR QUARTERS	(b) AVERAGE ANNUAL SALES OR RECEIPTS FOR PRECEDING THREE FISCAL YEARS

12. FLOOR SPACE (*Square feet*) | **13.** NET WORTH

MANUFACTURING	WAREHOUSE	DATE	AMOUNT

14. SECURITY CLEARANCE (*If applicable, check highest clearance authorized*)

	FOR	TOP SECRET	SECRET	CONFIDENTIAL	NAMES OF AGENCIES WHICH GRANTED SECURITY CLEARANCES (*Include dates*)
KEY PERSONNEL					
PLANT ONLY					

THIS SPACE FOR USE BY THE GOVERNMENT	CERTIFICATION
	I certify that information supplied herein (*Including all pages attached*) is correct and that neither the applicant nor any person (*Or concern*) in any connection with the applicant as a principal or officer, so far as is known, is now debarred or otherwise declared ineligible by any agency of the Federal Government from bidding for furnishing materials, supplies, or services to the Government or any agency thereof.
	SIGNATURE
	NAME AND TITLE OF PERSON AUTHORIZED TO SIGN (*Type or print*)

129–105

STANDARD FORM 129 (REV. 2–77)
Prescribed by GSA, FPR (41 CFR) 1–16.802

INFORMATION AND INSTRUCTIONS

Persons or concerns wishing to be added to a particular agency's bidder's mailing list for supplies or services shall file this properly completed and certified Bidder's Mailing List Application, together with such other lists as may be attached to this application form, with each procurement office of the Federal agency with which they desire to do business. If a Federal agency has attached a Supplemental Commodity List with instructions, complete the application as instructed. Otherwise, identify in item 8 the equipment, supplies and/or services on which you desire to bid. The application shall be submitted and signed by the principal as distinguished from an agent, however constituted.

After placement on the bidder's mailing list of an agency, a supplier's failure to respond (*submission of bid, or notice in writing, that you are unable to bid on that particular transaction but wish to remain on the active bidder's mailing list for that particular item*) to Invitations for Bids will be understood by the agency to indicate lack of interest and concurrence in the removal of the supplier's name from the purchasing activity's bidder's mailing list for the items concerned.

DEFINITION RELATING TO TYPE OF OWNERSHIP
(See *item 9*)

Minority business enterprise. A minority business enterprise is defined as a "business, at least 50 percent of which is owned by minority group members or, in case of publicly owned businesses, at least 51 percent of the stock of which is owned by minority group members." For the purpose of this definition, minority group members are Negroes, Spanish-speaking American persons, American-Orientals, American-Indians, American-Eskimos, and American-Aleuts.

TYPE OF BUSINESS DEFINITIONS
(See *item 10*)

a. Manufacturer or producer—means a person (or concern) owning, operating, or maintaining a store, warehouse, or other establishment that produces, on the premises, the materials, supplies, articles, or equipment of the general character of those listed in item 8, or in the Federal Agency's Supplemental Commodity List, if attached.

b. Regular dealer (Type 1)—means a person (or concern) who owns, operates, or maintains a store, warehouse, or other establishment in which the materials, supplies, articles, or equipment of the general character listed in item 8 or in the Federal Agency's Supplemental Commodity List, if attached, are bought, kept in stock, and sold to the public in the usual course of business.

c. Regular dealer (Type 2)—in the case of supplies of particular kinds (*at present, petroleum, lumber and timber products, machine tools, raw cotton, green coffee, hay, grain, feed, or straw, agricultural liming materials, tea, raw or unmanufactured cotton linters*). **Regular dealer**—means a person (or concern) satisfying the requirements of the regulations (Code of Federal Regulations, Title 41, 50–201.101(b)) as amended from time to time, prescribed by the Secretary of Labor under the Walsh-Healey Public Contracts Act (Title 41 U.S. Code 35–45). For coal dealers see Code of Federal Regulations, Title 41, 50–201.604(a).

d. Service establishment—means a concern (or person) which owns, operates, or maintains any type of business which is principally engaged in the furnishing of nonpersonal services, such as (*but not limited to*) repairing, cleaning, redecorating, or rental of personal property, including the furnishing of necessary repair parts or other supplies as part of the services performed.

e. Construction concern—means a concern (or person) engaged in construction, alteration or repair (including dredging, excavating, and painting) of buildings, structures, and other real property.

DEFINITIONS RELATING TO SIZE OF BUSINESS
(See *item 11*)

a. Small business concern—A small business concern for the purpose of Government procurement is a concern, including its affiliates, which is independently owned and operated, is not dominant in the field of operation in which it is bidding on Government contracts and can further qualify under the criteria concerning number of employees, average annual receipts, or other criteria, as prescribed by the Small Business Administration. (See Code of Federal Regulations, Title 13, Part 121, as amended, which contains detailed industry definitions and related procedures.)

b. Affiliates—Business concerns are affiliates of each other when either directly or indirectly (i) one concern controls or has the power to control the other, or (ii) a third party controls or has the power to control both. In determining whether concerns are independently owned and operated and whether or not affiliation exists, consideration is given to all appropriate factors including common ownership, common management, and contractual relationship. (See *items 6 and 11*.)

c. Number of employees—In connection with the determination of small business status, "number of employees" means the average employment of any concern, including the employees of its domestic and foreign affiliates, based on the number of persons employed on a full-time, part-time, temporary, or other basis during each of the pay periods of the preceding 12 months. If a concern has not been in existence for 12 months, "number of employees" means the average employment of such concern and its affiliates during the period that such concern has been in existence based on the number of persons employed during each of the pay periods of the period that such concern has been in business. (See *item 11*.)

● **COMMERCE BUSINESS DAILY**—The Commerce Business Daily, published by the Department of Commerce, contains information concerning proposed procurements, sales, and contract awards. For further information concerning this publication, contact your local Commerce Field Office.

Government Agencies

Both the General Services Administration and the Small Business Administration provide individuals and firms with detailed information about obtaining government contracts.

The *General Services Administration* serves as the purchasing agent for the federal government and is responsible for buying most of the products and services used by federal departments and agencies. To help businesses understand how the government's procurement system works, the GSA has established GSA Business Service Centers in several major cities. The business experts in these centers can provide you with:

- Detailed information about contracting opportunities, including those that have been set aside for small and disadvantaged businesses.
- Bidder's Mailing List applications.
- Copies of bid abstracts, indicating prices bid and who the successful bidders are.
- Publications designed to assist business representatives in doing business with the government.

GENERAL SERVICES ADMINISTRATION
BUSINESS SERVICE CENTERS

Director of Public Services
General Services
  Administration
18th & F Streets, N.W.,
  Room 6122
Washington, D.C. 20405
Tel: 202/566-1240

Central Office

Regional Director of Business
  Affairs
General Services
  Administration
John W. McCormick, Post
  Office and Courthouse
Boston, MA 02109
Tel: 617/233-2868

Region 1—Connecticut, Maine,
  Massachusetts, New
  Hampshire, Rhode Island,
  and Vermont

Regional Director of Business Affairs
General Services Administration
26 Federal Plaza
New York, NY 10007
Tel: 212/264-1234

Region 2—New Jersey, New York, Puerto Rico, and Virgin Islands

Regional Director of Business Affairs
General Services Administration
7th & D Streets, S.W.
Washington, D.C. 20407
Tel: 202/472-1804

Region 3—District of Columbia, Maryland, Virginia, and West Virginia

Manager, Mid-Atlantic Business Service Center
General Services Administration
600 Arch Street
Philadelphia, PA 19106
Tel: 215/597-9613

Region 3—Pennsylvania and Delaware

Regional Director of Business Affairs
General Services Administration
1776 Peachtree Street, N.W.
Atlanta, GA 30309
Tel: 404/526-5661

Region 4—Alabama, Florida, Georgia, Kentucky, Mississippi, North Carolina, South Carolina, and Tennessee

Regional Director of Business Affairs
General Services Administration
230 Dearborn Street
Chicago, IL 60604
Tel: 312/353-5383

Region 5—Illinois, Indiana, Michigan, Minnesota, Ohio and Wisconsin

Regional Director of Business Affairs
General Services Administration
1500 East Bannister Road
Kansas City, MO 64131
Tel: 816/926-7203

Region 6—Iowa, Kansas, Missouri, and Nebraska

Regional Director of Business
  Affairs
General Services
  Administration
819 Taylor Street
Fort Worth, TX 76102
Tel: 817/334-3284

Region 7—Arkansas,
  Louisiana, New Mexico,
  Oklahoma, and Texas

Manager, Gulf Coast Business
  Service Center
General Services
  Administration
Federal Office Building and
  Courthouse
515 Rusk Street
Houston, TX 77002
Tel: 713/226-5787

Region 7—Gulf Coast from
  Brownsville, Texas to New
  Orleans, Louisiana

Regional Director of Business
  Affairs
General Services
  Administration
Bldg. 41, Denver Federal
  Center
Denver, CO 80225
Tel: 303/234-4171

Region 8—Colorado, North
  Dakota, South Dakota,
  Montana, Utah, and
  Wyoming

Regional Director of Business
  Affairs
General Services
  Administration
525 Market Street
San Francisco, CA 94105
Tel: 415/556-0877

Region 9—Arizona, California,
  Hawaii, and Nevada

Manager, Business Service
  Center
General Services
  Administration
525 Market Street
San Francisco, CA 94105
Tel: 415/556-2122

Region 9—Northern
  California, Hawaii, and all of
  Nevada except Clark County

Manager, Business Service
Center
General Services
Administration
500 North Los Angeles
Los Angeles, CA 90012
Tel: 213/688-3210

Region 9—Los Angeles and
Southern California, Clark
County, Nevada, and
Arizona

Regional Director of Business
Affairs
General Services
Administration
440 Federal Building
915 Second Avenue
Seattle, WA 98174
Tel: 206/442-5556

Region 10—Alaska, Idaho,
Oregon, and Washington

The *Small Business Administration* wants to see that small businesses receive their fair share of government contracts. To accomplish this, the SBA works closely with government agencies to develop procurement policies and procedures that will increase the number of contracts awarded to small-business concerns. SBA procurement center representatives (PCRs) are stationed at all federal installations, both military and civilian, that have major buying programs. The PCR's job is to make sure that small businesses are not being excluded from the contracting process and to try to obtain "small-business set-asides" whenever possible. Competition for contracts designated as small-business set-asides is restricted to small businesses only; large businesses are not permitted to submit bids or proposals.

In addition to helping small businesses win government contracts, the SBA helps them win subcontracting assignments by working with prime contractors to ensure that they use qualified small businesses as subcontractors on government projects. In this regard, SBA subcontracting specialists regularly visit large government contractors and make the capabilities of small businesses known to them.

To facilitate the match-up between small businesses and the government agencies and major contractors who can

Is this an updated profile form?   Yes ☐ No ☐

PROCUREMENT **A**UTOMATED **S**OURCE **S**YSTEM — **COMPANY PROFILE**

IDENTIFICATION PASS is designed only for small businesses which are organized for profit and independently owned and operated

COMPANY NAME _____

_____

MAILING ADDRESS _____

CITY _____ STATE _____ ZIP _____

CONTACT PERSON _____ TITLE _____

EMPLOYER IDENTIFICATION NO. (if avail.) _____

NO. OF EMPLOYEES _____

TOTAL SALES LAST FISCAL YEAR _____

YEAR BUSINESS ESTABLISHED _____

PHONE _ _ _ _   _ _ _ _   _ _ _ _
                Area Code   Number

PASS is divided into 4 types of businesses. Please estimate the percentage of your business allocated to the following (total must equal 100%) and complete the appropriate section(s).

MANUFACTURING/SUPPLIES [%]

CHECK ONE ☑

☐ MANUFACTURER   ☐ DEALER   ☐ WHOLESALE DISTRIBUTOR
   MANUFACTURING FACILITY   SIZE _____ SQ. FT

CONSTRUCTION [%]

MAXIMUM CURRENT BONDING LEVEL $_____
                                        (if applicable)
MAXIMUM OPERATING RADIUS _____ MILES
ANYWHERE IN U.S., ENTER 3999 ABOVE
ANYWHERE IN THE WORLD. ENTER 9999 ABOVE

RESEARCH and DEVELOPMENT [%]

No. of engineers & scientists _____
Expertise of key personnel _____
_____
_____

SERVICES [%]

MAXIMUM CURRENT BONDING LEVEL $_____
                                        (if applicable)
MAXIMUM OPERATING RADIUS _____ MILES
ANYWHERE IN U.S. ENTER 3999 ABOVE
ANYWHERE IN THE WORLD. ENTER 9999 ABOVE

CAPABILITIES (limit 32 words — avoid abbreviations)

List products and services offered and special capabilities
_____
_____
_____
_____
_____

OWNERSHIP CHECK **ALL** APPLICABLE BOXES ☑

Company is at least
51% OWNED, CONTROLLED
and **ACTIVELY MANAGED BY:**

☐ VETERAN(S)
☐ CHECK IF ANY SERVICE WAS
   IN VIETNAM ERA (1964-1975)
☐ WOMAN/WOMEN
☐ MINORITY PERSON(S)

IF MINORITY OWNER. CHECK ☑

☐ BLACK AMERICAN   ☐ HISPANIC AMERICAN
☐ NATIVE AMERICAN   ☐ ASIAN PACIFIC AMERICAN
   American Indian,   (Includes Oriental)
   Eskimo, Aleut & Native
   Hawaiian)

EXPORTS CHECK **ONE** BOX ☑ FOR INTERNATIONAL TRADE INTEREST

☐ ACTIVE EXPORTER   ☐ INTERESTED IN EXPORTS   ☐ NOT INTERESTED IN EXPORTS

SIGNATURE Important! Signature is required!

INFORMATION CONTAINED IN THIS PROFILE MAY BE DISCLOSED AT THE DISCRETION OF THE SMALL BUSINESS ADMINISTRATION

Please sign here
↘

_____   _____   _____ |_____|
Signature of Company Officer   Title   Date   (for SBA Use)

Questions? Contact your regional or district U.S. Small Business Administration Office for answers.

SBA Form 1167 A (5-82)
Prev. Editions Obsolete
OMB Approved: 3245-0024

benefit from their services, the SBA has developed the *Procurement Automated Source System (PASS)*. PASS is designed to provide agencies and contractors with profiles of small businesses who are potential bidders on contracts or subcontracts. By having your consulting firm computer-listed on the PASS roster, you can broaden your exposure and gain valuable information about contract offerings. To be included in PASS, all you need to do is fill out a "Company Profile" form and mail it back to the SBA. Copies of the form can be obtained from SBA field offices (see Chapter 9 for the addresses).

Government Publications

Each of the government publications described here can provide you with additional information about selling your consulting services to the government.

- "Commerce Business Daily." This publication is published Monday through Friday by the Department of Commerce. It lists civilian agency and military procurement invitations, subcontracting leads, contract awards, sales of surplus property, and foreign business opportunities. If you are serious about doing business with the government, this publication is a must. Copies are available at SBA field offices, GSA Business Service Centers, and many public libraries. Subscriptions can be obtained through the Superintendent of Documents, Government Printing Office, Washington, D.C. 20402.
- "Handbook for Small Business: A Survey of Small Business Programs of the Federal Government." This publication contains information on government purchasing and sales programs, government-sponsored loans, financial guarantees and grants, and management and training assistance programs. In addition to describing each program, it tells how and where further information can be found. The publication is for sale by the Superintendent of Documents, Government Printing Office.

- "Selling to the Military." Here, you can obtain addresses and telephone numbers of major buying offices of the army, navy, air force, and Defense Logistics Agency. It summarizes the procurement responsibilities and purchases of each office and gives advice on how to make your capabilities known. The publication is for sale by the Superintendent of Documents, Government Printing Office, or may be obtained from Department of Defense contracting offices.
- "Selling to the U.S. Government." This publication explains government buying methods, how to locate purchasing agencies, what they buy, how to have an opportunity to bid on government contracts and prepare bids and proposals. It is available free of charge from the Small Business Administration.
- "U.S. Government Purchasing and Sales Directory." This directory provides a listing of products and services bought by all federal agencies, keyed to the purchasing offices that buy them. You can obtain it from the Small Business Administration.
- "Washington, D.C., Federal Buying Directory." Here you'll find a comprehensive listing of federal officials in the Washington, D.C., area who either buy or have knowledge of the buying done by their agencies. Copies are available from the General Services Administration.

Public Notices

Another way that the government informs potential bidders of contract offerings is through public notices. These notices are often placed in newspapers, trade and professional publications, and government bulletins released by various agencies. Notices are also sent to individuals who have expressed an interest in being considered for specific types of contracts.

TIPS FOR SELLING YOUR SERVICES

1. Determine which government agencies are most likely to need the type of consulting services you can provide.
2. Focus your selling efforts on the best prospects, securing placement on each agency's Bidder's Mailing List.
3. List your consulting firm on the SBA's PASS roster so that government agencies and contractors can be made aware of your capabilities.
4. Respond to each Invitation for Bids or Request for Proposals that you receive, thereby maintaining your status on the corresponding Bidder's Mailing Lists.
5. Increase your success rate by making sure that your bids or proposals meet the requirements of each IFB or RFP.
6. Don't overlook subcontracting opportunities; once a major contract has been awarded, contact the winning consulting firm to express your interest in working on the assignment.
7. Get to know the contracting officers of the various departments and agencies; whenever possible, make personal visits to their offices on a regular basis.

11

Generating Additional Income

IN ADDITION to the basic consulting services that you provide, there are a number of other ways to market your knowledge and expertise. Speaking, conducting seminars, writing articles, publishing newsletters, and producing training materials are just a few of the ways you can earn additional income. In some instances the income generated by these "fringe" activities can even exceed that from consulting activities.

SOURCES OF INCOME

Each of the activities or products discussed below represents another source of income that is available to consultants.

Selling Supplies or Merchandise

One of the most logical and lucrative ways that consultants can generate additional income is through the sale of related supplies and merchandise. Interior designers and space planners, for example, often obtain the furnishings and fixtures that are required for a project, then charge the client for the purchase cost plus a percentage mark-up. Security-systems consultants not only advise clients on how to guard against intruders and prevent property losses but also provide them with the security devices to do the job. A physical-fitness consultant might market a line of exercise equipment or sportswear. Time-management consultants can sell datebooks, calendars, and forms specifically designed to aid clients and others in implementing their time-management techniques.

Writing Computer Programs

Computer programs that enable customers to have instant access to a consultant's decision-making ability or other skills have become a steadily growing source of income for many consultants. Even if you are not in a computer-related field, you may still be able to use this method to package your knowledge by working together with a computer software designer to develop programs that will meet the needs of your intended customers. For instance, a financial planner might sell a program that analyzes stocks for investors. A marketing consultant could create a program that identifies sales trends.

Public Speaking

Public speaking is a way to enhance both your bank balance and your reputation. Experts in such diverse fields as human relations, inventory control, gourmet cooking, taxes, entrepreneurship, communications, stress management, personal selling, and wardrobe planning are finding ready audiences for their presentations. Noncelebrity speakers are routinely paid between $500 and $2,500 to deliver a one-hour talk at a luncheon or dinner meeting. Celebrities who are already well known to their audiences can earn upward of $15,000. Along with the speaking fee and expenses that you receive, there's the opportunity to come into contact with prospective clients.

Launching yourself as a professional speaker isn't as difficult as you might think. You can do it through your own promotional efforts or through the services of a lecture bureau, which will handle bookings for you in exchange for 30 to 40 percent of your fee. If you opt to do it yourself, the following suggestions should help you to get started:

1. Build up your confidence and hone your speaking skills by volunteering to speak for free in the beginning.
2. Contact the program chairpersons of the local business and civic organizations whose members are most likely to benefit from your information. The Rotary Club, Business and Professional Women's Club, PTA, Chamber of Commerce, Kiwanis, and similar groups all have ongoing needs for speakers.
3. Describe the talk that you are prepared to give and offer to speak at an upcoming meeting.
4. Make audiocassette recordings of your speeches so that you can evaluate them later. They can also be used as audition tapes.
5. Get in touch with the producers of local radio and television talk shows that reach the people you want to reach and let them know that you have information that might be of interest to their audiences. This can be done via the telephone, but you should follow it up by sending a letter and your résumé.
6. Put together a brochure that describes your background and the various topics on which you are qualified to speak.
7. List yourself in one or more speakers directories that program chairpersons and corporate executives use to select speakers. One directory in which you may want to be included is *The Directory of Speakers* (Oryx Press, 2214 N. Central, Phoenix, Arizona 85004). It contains the names, addresses, phone numbers, topics, and fee requirements of speakers throughout the United States.

Once you've developed your presentation and gained some experience in speaking to an audience, you are ready to go after paid speaking engagements. Here your best prospects include: trade and professional associations, corporations, convention bureaus, unions, and government agencies.

To locate lecture bureaus that represent speakers in your particular field, look in the Yellow Pages under "Lecture Bureaus" or "Booking Agents." For additional information, read *Speakers and Lecturers: How to Find Them,* edited by Paul Wasserman and Jacqueline R. Bernero (Gale Research Company, Book Tower, Detroit, Michigan 48226). This book provides the names and addresses of booking agents and lecture bureaus throughout the United States, along with details about the speakers they represent, subjects covered, and booking arrangements.

Giving Seminars

Another way to generate additional income is by conducting seminars. Instead of waiting to be invited to speak at a luncheon or dinner meeting, you can plan and promote your own event. In this case, you would handle all the arrangements, from finding an appropriate location in which to hold the seminar to sending out direct-mail brochures and/or placing ads in local newspapers.

The Seminar Format

Depending on its topic, audience, and price, a seminar can last anywhere from three hours to one or more days. You may be the sole presenter or one member of a panel of guest speakers. Some seminars are structured so that participants have a maximum opportunity for interaction with the seminar leader; others are structured more like lectures with a question-and-answer session at the end. Refreshments are optional. The most elaborate formats call for coffee and sweet rolls in the morning, lunch during the afternoon break, and beverage service throughout the day. For evening seminars or those lasting less than four hours it isn't necessary to serve refreshments, although coffee and ice water are always welcome.

Facilities and Costs

There are a number of locations where you can hold seminars—for instance, hotels, conference centers, auditoriums, colleges and universities, public buildings, community meeting rooms in shopping malls, banks, churches, even department stores (in conjunction with a special promotion). Some creative seminar planners even offer their seminars on cruise ships and airplanes. Based on the number of participants who will be attending the seminar, you might be able to hold it in your office or home. One publishing consultant we know of holds a three-part series of evening seminars in her penthouse apartment and serves wine and cheese to the participants.

The cost to stage and promote a seminar can range from less than $500 to more than $10,000. The factors that will determine your total cost are:

- Facility rental cost
- Refreshment cost
- Materials cost
- Promotion cost

You should be able to rent an average-size meeting room (one that seats up to fifty people) for somewhere between $30 and $100 per day. A larger room or auditorium would be more expensive. Hotels and conference centers will frequently provide free meeting space if you order a certain number of lunches or dinners. In this case, they make their profits from the meal service rather than from the facility rental.

Some hotels provide beverage service (coffee and ice water) at no extra charge, including it in the price of the meeting room. Others price it separately, charging $5 to $7 for each pot of coffee that you serve and a flat fee of $5 to $10 for ice water. If you provide lunch or dinner as part of the seminar, you'll probably spend between $10 and $20 per person. The items on the menu and the type of meal service you choose (sit-down or buffet) will largely determine the cost.

You must also ask yourself what seminar materials or handouts the participants will receive. The costs of producing any workbooks, audiocassettes, kits, supplies, or other materials you plan to give participants must all be included in your total cost. Some consultants keep their costs low by limiting each handout to just a few stapled-together pages. Others provide attractively bound workbooks and packaged sets of audiocassettes. Generally, you should wait until you have successfully conducted enough seminars to know the participants' needs before investing the time and money to create any elaborate materials.

Promotion is likely to comprise the largest expenditure of your total seminar cost. The two most widely used methods of seminar promotion are direct mail and newspaper advertising, used separately or in combination. For the best results, though, it pays to know your target market. The more accurately you can pinpoint which prospects will be the most receptive to your seminar offering, the better your response will be. Once you have identified your best prospects, you can determine which media to use and what advertising message will be the most effective. When your best prospects are concentrated in a particular industry, group, occupation, or other category, direct mail tends to be the most effective means of reaching them. Its high degree of selectivity enables you to get your advertising materials into the right hands. If you are trying to reach a diverse audience that is less easily identifiable (such as people in need of financial advice), newspaper advertising is the best method to use. For more information on promotion techniques, see Chapter 5.

Seminar Fees

Your seminar fee must be high enough to cover your costs and provide a sufficient amount of profit. A three-hour seminar can cost anywhere from $25 to $100 per person, while an all-day seminar can run from $50 to $300. One way to determine a fee is to set a goal for the total revenues you wish to generate from the seminar. Then divide that figure by the estimated number of people who will take the seminar. The result is the fee you need to charge. If the seminar fee seems too high in comparison with the competition, you can try to either attract more participants or lower your revenues goal, thereby reducing your fee.

Teaching

Based on your professional experience and academic background, it's possible that you are qualified to teach classes at the college or university level. Community colleges, state colleges and universities, and private schools often augment their full-time teaching staffs with part-time instructors who are knowledgeable in specialized fields. From the school's point of view, hiring outsiders on a part-time basis keeps instructional costs low and gives students access to teachers with current, first-hand experience in their fields of expertise. This arrangement is also advantageous from the part-time teacher's point of view. In addition to being a personally satisfying experience, teaching (1) adds professional credibility, (2) provides an opportunity to polish speaking and presentation skills, and (3) creates additional income.

The prerequisites for becoming a part-time instructor vary from state to state and from one school to another. Depending on the subject area, a master's degree and two years' professional experience may be required, or professional experience alone may be sufficient. When it comes to teaching classes in vocational studies and fine arts, the emphasis is usually on professional experience. Other departments, such as English, history, math, and science, place greater emphasis on academic credentials. Part-time instructors' salaries, which are generally set at an hourly rate, range from $15 to $50 per hour.

Selling Audiocassettes

Another means of packaging and presenting your knowledge is through audiocassettes. They can be sold in conjunction with speaking engagements and seminars or by direct mail. Audiocassettes are particularly appealing to salespersons and business executives who are on the road a lot and want to make productive use of their driving time. The greatest demand is for self-help cassettes on such subjects as time management, positive thinking, selling techniques, communications skills, and real estate investments.

A major advantage of selling audiocassettes is their high profit margin. A single sixty-minute cassette typically sells for $15 to $20. A package of 4 to 8 cassettes can sell for $60 to $150 or more. The actual unit cost, though, is usually a small fraction of the sales price. For instance, the cost to manufacture 100 to 250 sixty-minute cassettes is approximately $2 per unit plus $50 to $75 per hour for studio production time. This includes labeling and packaging costs. The larger your order, the lower your unit costs will be. To locate production studios in your area, check the Yellow Pages under "Audio Visual Production Services" or "Tapes."

Selling Videocassettes

Rock musicians aren't the only ones who have discovered the power of videotape. Many consultants who have been successful in marketing seminars and audiocassettes are now turning to videocassettes as an alternative medium for reaching their audiences. In this way the purchaser of the cassette can *see* your presentation, viewing it as often as desired at his or her convenience. Although a videocassette is considerably more expensive to produce than an audiocassette, it also fetches a much higher sales price. A thirty-minute videocassette generally sells for anywhere from $40 to $300. The simpler your video production is, the less it will cost. A one-camera setup, in which you are the sole actor and only a few special effects are used, will be less expensive than a three-camera setup with several actors, different sets, and numerous special effects. For more details about producing videocassettes, contact the production studios in your area. You should also check with the television stations (local and cable), since they often lease out their production facilities and crews.

Writing Articles

Close to 9,500 newspapers and over 60,000 magazines are currently published in the United States. These numbers include daily and weekly newspapers and consumer and trade magazines. Given the need to provide their readers with the most up-to-date and thorough information available, the majority of these publications accept articles written by free-lance writers. Depending on the topic and the writer's reputation, a fifteen-hundred-word article (approximately six typewritten pages) can sell for between $175 and $1,000.

When it comes to selecting a topic, writing experts generally advise that you write about something you know. Thus, a marketing consultant might choose to write about such topics as:

Advertising	Pricing
Brand names	Product development
Consumer behavior	Shipping methods
Distribution	Trends and fashions
Packaging	

Any one of these topics could result in a wealth of articles directed at marketing professionals or the general public. For instance, the topic "Advertising" might yield these articles:

- "How Advertisers Convince You to Buy"
- "Subliminal Selling—Does It Work?"
- "Tailoring Your Ads to the Foreign Market"
- "Choosing an Ad Agency"
- "Measuring the Effectiveness of Your Ads"
- "What the Ads Don't Tell You"
- "Madison Avenue Imagemakers"
- "Advertising Jingles Keep Cash Registers Ringing"
- "TV Networks Vie for Advertisers' Dollars"
- "How Susceptible Are You to Advertising?"

Before you sit down at the typewriter (or word processor) and begin to write an article, it's a good idea to spend some time thinking about who will publish it. Rather than writing an article and sending the finished manuscript to prospective publishers, it's usually better to send a query letter first. A query letter describes the article you intend to write and explains why it will be of interest to the publication's readers. At the same time, it should highlight your qualifications, emphasizing that you have the background and experience to write the proposed article.

From the editor's point of view, the advantages of sending a query letter over a manuscript are that (1) a query letter can be read quickly, and (2) if the idea appeals to the editor, he or she can work with the writer to develop the right approach for the article. From the writer's point of view, the advantages are that (1) it takes less time to write a query letter than to write an entire article, (2) a query letter stands a better chance of being read (unsolicited manuscripts are often returned unopened), and (3) editors usually respond more quickly to query letters.

Once you've sold an editor on your idea, then you can proceed to write the article, tailoring it to meet the needs of the publication in which it will appear.

To give your finished manuscript a professional appearance, be sure to:

1. Type it neatly on 8½ × 11" white paper (20 lb. weight). Never use erasable or onion-skin paper since these are flimsier and editors find them difficult to handle.
2. Type the title of your article in the upper left-hand corner of the first page; on separate lines below this, type your name, address, phone number, and the length of the manuscript (_____ words).
3. Start the first line of copy approximately one-third of the way down the first page.
4. Double-space your copy, leaving a one-inch margin on all sides of the page.
5. Number each page (except the first) in the upper right-hand corner; along with the number put your last name and a shortened form of the title ("How Advertisers Convince You to Buy" might be written "Advertisers Convince").
6. Type one of the following notations on the last page of

your manuscript below the last line of copy: ###, -30-, The End. This lets the editor know that there is no additional material to follow.

7. Use a paper clip, rather than a staple, to hold your manuscript pages together; this is more convenient for the editor.

Once your article is ready to send out to a newspaper or magazine, prepare a *cover letter* to go with it. Your cover letter should set forth your reasons for submitting the article to the publication, why the article is of value, and the professional background that qualifies you to write it. If you previously sent a query letter to the publication and were told to go ahead and write the article, make a note of this in your cover letter ("Per your request, enclosed is my article 'How Advertisers Convince You to Buy.' As you may recall from the query letter I sent you in June, this article is about . . .").

Last, but not least, don't forget to enclose a self-addressed stamped envelope (SASE) with your manuscript. This will ensure its safe return to you if, for some reason, the publication is unable to use it. Some writers feel that enclosing an SASE is inviting failure by assuming from the start that the manuscript will be rejected. This isn't the case. Enclosing an SASE shows that you have a professional approach toward your writing and are aware of the rules of publishing etiquette.

Publishing Reports

Another way to combine your consulting expertise and writing talents is by publishing reports. A report can be anywhere from a few pages in length to more than a hundred, held together by a staple or presented in an attractive binder. Its purpose is to convey current information that will enable the purchaser of the report to take a course of action. For instance, an insurance consultant might prepare a forty-page report aimed at the owners and managers of medium-size businesses. Entitled "How to Keep Your Company's Insurance Costs Down," it would provide the reader with a step-by-step plan for setting up an improved program of risk management. A real estate consultant could put together a fifteen-page report, "Your Dream House—How to Find It, How to Buy It," designed to help prospective home buyers make the right decisions.

The price that a customer is willing to pay for a report depends on how badly he or she wants the information. The quality and the relevance of the information are what counts, not the number of pages. You can charge more for a twenty-page report on a high-interest subject than for an eighty-page report on a low-interest subject. Generally, you should be able to sell a twenty-page report for $10 to $25. If the information is particularly timely or would be difficult to obtain by other means, your price could be considerably higher.

Publishing Newsletters

One source of income that seems ideally suited to consultants is newsletter publishing. Like consultants' services, newsletters provide clients with information and assistance on an ongoing basis. Newsletters inform readers about the changes occurring in a particular field and/or advise what steps they should take to accomplish specific goals. By gathering information from a variety of news sources (the media, industry leaders, bankers, stock analysts, and so on) and condensing it into a few pages, newsletters save the reader time. By drawing attention to key facts or interpreting the reasons behind recent developments, newsletters help the reader to make decisions.

The more frequently you publish your newsletter, the more time-consuming and costly it will be to produce. Some newsletters are published weekly; others on a biweekly, monthly, or quarterly basis. In the beginning at least, you should stick to a monthly or quarterly schedule. Later, after you've learned a few publishing shortcuts, you can increase the frequency of issues if the demand warrants it. Another factor to consider is the size of your newsletter. This can range from two pages (one 8½ × 11″ sheet of paper printed on both sides) to more than twenty pages. The most common size for a newsletter, though, is four pages (one 8½ × 17" sheet of paper printed on both sides and folded in half).

Newsletter prices, like report prices, are determined by how valuable their information is to readers. Some newsletters cost as little as $15 for a one-year subscription, while others cost $1,000 or more. Those in the latter category include a few investment newsletters as well as newsletters whose primary subscribers are corporations.

Writing Books

One of the most satisfying ways to generate additional income is by writing books. Along with the financial rewards and professional recognition that you can derive from writing books, they provide an opportunity to present readers with an in-depth view of your subject.

There are two basic methods to get your book published: (1) You can sell it to an independent publishing house in much the same way as you would sell an article, or (2) you can publish it yourself. If you choose the first method, you will have the benefit of the publishing house's editorial and marketing expertise and won't have to invest your own money to produce the book. At the same time, though, you won't have control over the price of the book or how it is promoted. The second method, known as "self-publishing," gives you the greatest degree of control, but it also entails the most risk. In addition to financing the publishing project yourself, you must find a reputable printer to typeset, print, and bind the book. Then it's up to you to market it, using such means as direct mail, book wholesalers, seminars and the like.

To find out more about writing and publishing, we recommend that you read the following publications:

Books

Getting Published: A Guide for Business People and Other Professionals, Gary S. Belkin, John Wiley & Sons, New York.
How to Get Happily Published, Judith Appelbaum and Nancy Evans, Harper and Row, New York.

How to Write Articles That Sell, L. Perry Wilbur, John Wiley & Sons, New York.

How to Write Books That Sell, L. Perry Wilbur, Contemporary Books, Chicago.

International Directory of Little Magazines and Small Presses, P.O. Box 100, Paradise, California 95969.

Literary Market Place, R. R. Bowker, New York, annual. Lists magazines, newspapers, book clubs, agents, reviewers, and a variety of related services.

Publishers, Distributors and Wholesalers of the United States, R. R. Bowker, New York, annual. Lists major publishers, distributors, wholesalers, small presses, associations that act as publishers, and software publishers.

The Self-Publishing Handbook, David M. Brownstone and Irene M. Franck, New American Library, New York.

The Self-Publishing Manual: How to Write, Print & Sell Your Own Book, Para Publishing, P.O. Box 4232, Santa Barbara, Calif.

Ulrich's International Periodicals Directory, R. R. Bowker, New York, annual. Lists thousands of periodicals.

Working Press of the Nation. National Research Bureau, Burlington, Iowa, annual. Lists newspapers, magazines, feature writers, editors, and addresses.

Writer's Market, Writer's Digest, Cincinnati, Ohio, annual. Lists the places where you can sell any kind of writing— articles, nonfiction books, novels, short stories, scripts, and more. It tells you the names and addresses of editors, how much they are paying, and what their editorial needs are.

Magazines

Publishers Weekly, 1911 Rowland Street, Riverton, New Jersey.

Writer's Digest, 9933 Alliance Road, Cincinnati, Ohio.

12

Recordkeeping and Taxes

As AN independent consultant, it is essential for you to maintain good financial records. The most obvious reason for this is that the more accurate and up-to-date your records are, the easier it will be to prepare your income tax returns. There are other reasons as well. Along with the need to keep good records to satisfy the government, you also need them for your own benefit. Setting up an efficient recordkeeping system is the best way to ensure that you receive all of the business-related tax deductions to which you are entitled. It also should go a long way toward pleasing your clients, since you will have fewer billing errors. In addition, by helping you to recognize problems or opportunities quickly, your records can be a valuable tool in making business decisions. Good records enable you to substitute facts for guesswork, continuity for confusion. Instead of having to hunt for the financial information you need or develop it on the spot, you already have it in hand ready to be used.

INFORMATION YOUR RECORDS SHOULD PROVIDE

Your recordkeeping system should include information on:

• Monthly income totals
• Business operating expenses

- Accounts receivable totals
- Financial obligations coming due
- Current sources of income
- Services or products most in demand
- Who your best clients are
- Clients behind on their bills
- Money invested in supplies and inventory
- Total value of your assets
- Overall profitability

This information, which is necessary for tax reporting and management purposes, is also likely to be required by any lending institutions, suppliers, and others with whom you do business.

CHOOSING A RECORDKEEPING SYSTEM

The Internal Revenue Service does not stipulate what kind of records a business owner must keep, only that the records properly document the business's income, expenses, and deductions. Thus you may use any recordkeeping system that meets this criterion and is suited to your consulting practice. For best results, the system you choose should be (1) simple to use, (2) easy to understand, (3) accurate, (4) consistent, and (5) capable of providing timely information.

You can choose from among a number of business recordkeeping systems ranging from the traditional double-entry system used by accountants to the simpler single-entry and pegboard systems available at stationery and business-forms stores.

Double-Entry Recordkeeping System

The double-entry recordkeeping system is the most difficult to use of the various systems. But, because of its built-in checks and balances, it provides the greatest degree of accuracy. At the same time, it has the capacity to provide a greater amount of financial information than the other systems. Based on the balance sheet for your business, it requires you to make two entries for every transaction that is recorded, since all transactions involve an exchange of one thing for another. For instance, if a client pays cash for an audiocassette or other merchandise that you sell, the amount of money in your consulting practice increases while your inventory level decreases. Under the double-entry system, you must record both changes in your books—one as a debit entry and the other as a credit entry. This is where the checks and balances come in. For each transaction, the total debit amount must always equal the total credit amount. If the amounts are out of balance, the transaction has been improperly recorded.

Single-Entry Recordkeeping System

The single-entry recordkeeping system differs from the double-entry in that it is based on your income statement, rather than your balance sheet. In this respect, it doesn't require you to "balance the books" or record more than one entry for each transaction. The simplicity of the system is its best feature and what makes it so appealing to the owners of new or small businesses. For tax purposes, the system enables you quickly and easily to record the flow of income and expenses generated by your consulting practice. In addition to this, a good single-entry recordkeeping system provides a means of keeping track of your accounts receivable, accounts payable, depreciable assets, and inventory. An accountant or bookkeeper can set up a system especially tailored to the needs of your practice, or you may find that one of the commercially available, ready-made systems meets your requirements. Generally consisting of worksheets bound together in a spiral notebook, these systems can be purchased at office-supply and stationery stores. The most popular single-entry system currently on the market is the one put out by Dome Publishing Company.

Pegboard Recordkeeping System

The pegboard recordkeeping system is actually a single-entry system since it requires only one entry per business transaction. But its unique design puts it in a category by itself. For one thing, it is an all-in-one system that not only keeps track of your records but provides the materials for writing checks and issuing receipts. The system derives its name from its format, in which checks and receipts are overlaid, one after another, on top of your permanent record sheets and held in place by pegs. Whenever you write a check or receipt, the information is automatically transferred, via carbon paper, to the record sheet below. This is the system's most distinguishing feature, because it eliminates the cause of most accounting errors: forgetting to enter a transaction in the books. For more information on pegboard systems, check the Yellow Pages under "Business Forms and Systems" to locate the pegboard system specialists near you.

Accountants and Bookkeepers

To determine which kind of recordkeeping system is the most suitable for your consulting practice, we strongly recommend that you talk to an accountant. An accountant can help you choose the right system and set it up properly. Once the system is in place, you and the accountant should plan to meet at periodic intervals throughout the year to make sure your records are in order and to evaluate your current financial position. To handle the day-to-day aspects of recordkeeping, you may also wish to use the services of a part-time bookkeeper. This will, of course, depend on the extent of your accounting or bookkeeping experience and the amount of time you have available to spend on recordkeeping activities. Many consultants have a bookkeeper come in once a week or every other week, as needed, to do their books.

RECORDING YOUR INCOME

One of the most important functions of your recordkeeping system is to provide an accurate record of the sources and

amounts of income generated by your consulting practice—
essential not only for tax-reporting purposes but also for
decision-making. At the bare minimum, income records for
your consulting practice must include a cash receipts journal
and an accounts receivable journal.

Cash Receipts Journal

The cash receipts journal on page 161 illustrates how a
consulting firm (in this case, a marketing research firm) can
simply and easily keep track of its income flow. Recording
the date, source, and amount of income earned, the cash
receipts journal also indicates which services are most in
demand. Thus, in addition to providing you with the income
figures required by the IRS, it provides valuable information
about your target market—the types of clients who are your
best prospects. After a few months of recording your cash
receipts in this way, you should know who your best clients
are and which of your services are generating the most
income.

The marketing research consultant offers a variety of
services: market share analysis, product research, advertising effectiveness evaluations, and consumer behavior studies. Yet the cash receipts journal shows that the income from
market share analysis far exceeds the income from any of the
other consulting services. This is a good example of what
marketing experts call the 80/20 Rule. According to the rule,
80 percent of a business's sales are likely to come from 20
percent of its customers (in this example, clients in the
packaged-food industry). These are your best prospects, the
clients who can most benefit from your services. Once you've
identified them, you should direct your promotional, selling,
and client-relations efforts toward filling their needs.

Accounts Receivable Journal

An accounts receivable journal, such as the one on page 161,
serves much the same purpose as a cash receipts journal.
Instead of showing the income you have already collected,

FERRIS AND ASSOCIATES
APRIL 19XX
CASH RECEIPTS JOURNAL

DATE	DESCRIPTION/NAME	ADVERTISING EVALUATION	CONSUMER BEHAVIOR	MARKET SHARE ANALYSIS	PRODUCT RESEARCH
4/1	Amalgamated Bakers			3000 00	
4/15	RPM Industries		1000 00		
4/20	Foremost Foods			2500 00	
4/30	Sierra Construction				2000 00

FERRIS AND ASSOCIATES
ACCOUNTS RECEIVABLE JOURNAL

DATE DUE	DESCRIPTION/NAME	DATE REC'D	AMOUNT DUE	30 DAYS PAST DUE	60 DAYS PAST DUE	90 DAYS PAST DUE
3/15	Stevens Corporation		1000 00	✓	✓	
4/21	Foremost Foods	4/20	2500 00	-	-	-
4/30	Sierra Construction	4/30	2000 00	-	-	-
5/17	Tanney Industries		4000 00			

FERRIS AND ASSOCIATES
APRIL 19XX
CASH DISBURSEMENTS JOURNAL

DATE	DESCRIPTION/NAME	CK#	ACCOUNTING	ADVERTISING	AUTOMOBILE	UTILITIES
4/3	Mel Louis, C.P.A.	645	6 5 0 00			
4/7	Daily Times	646		4 0 0 00		
4/9	Auto Dealer	647			7 5 0 0	
4/13	Electric Company	648				4 5 0 0

FERRIS AND ASSOCIATES
LIST OF DEPRECIABLE ASSETS

DATE	DESCRIPTION	COST	CLASS OF PROPERTY	DEPR. METHOD	DATE SOLD
1/16	Typewriter	1 2 5 0 00	5 y r s.		
2/15	Automobile	1 5 1 8 5 00	3 y r s.		
3/22	Computer	4 2 5 0 00	5 y r s.		
4/14	Telephone Answering Device	2 2 5 00	5 y r s.		

though, it shows the money that is owed to you by clients, enabling you to keep track of outstanding accounts and to determine which clients are behind in their bills. Then when you receive payment, you can enter the income in your cash receipts journal.

BUSINESS EXPENSES

The recordkeeping system for your consulting practice must provide you with a record of tax-deductible business expenses. So you will have to determine in advance precisely what expenses legitimately can be termed "business expenses." The Internal Revenue Services regards as deductible only those expenses that are "ordinary in your business and necessary for its operation." Here are just a few of the expenses that meet these criteria:

Accounting Services	Maintenance
Advertising	Materials
Attorneys' fees	Membership fees
Automobile	Messenger service
Business publications	Postage
Charitable contributions	Publicity
Consultants' fees	Rent
Credit reports	Safe deposit box
Depreciation	Seminars
Entertainment	Stationery
Freight charges	Supplies
Insurance	Taxes
Interest	Travel
Licenses	Utilities

In calculating your business expenses, it's important to separate them from your personal expenses. For example, if you go on a trip for both business and pleasure, you can deduct only the business portion of the trip. If you decide to extend your stay for a vacation or make a nonbusiness side trip, you may not deduct the additional expenses. Along this same vein, if your spouse accompanies you on a business trip, normally you would not be permitted to deduct his or her expenses for travel, meals, and lodging. (The exception to this would be if you can prove that your spouse's presence serves a real business purpose.)

Cash Disbursements Journal

The best way to keep track of your expenses is to enter them in a cash disbursements journal like the one shown on page 162. In so doing, make sure to record the following information:

• Date the expense was paid
• Name of person or business receiving payment
• Check number
• Amount of check
• Category of business expense

When you set up your expense categories, arrange them in either alphabetical order or the order in which they will appear on your tax forms. This will make it easier for you to locate the information later and transfer it to your tax forms when preparing your income tax return. At the end of each month, it's also a good idea to add up the expenses in each category to determine exactly where your money is going. This should help you to stay within your budget and keep unnecessary expenses to a minimum.

Automobile Expenses

If you use any automobiles or trucks in your consulting practice, those expenses resulting from the business use of the vehicles are deductible, including gasoline, oil, maintenance and repairs, insurance, depreciation, interest on car payments, parking fees, taxes, license fees, and tolls. When a motor vehicle is used for both business and personal purposes, you must divide your expenses between business and personal use.

There are two ways to calculate your deductible automobile expenses: (1) using a standard mileage rate, and (2) deducting a percentage of the total operating costs.

Standard Mile Rate

To calculate your deductible expenses using this method, keep a record of all the miles you drive for business reasons during the year. Then multiply your total business mileage times twenty-and-one-half cents per mile. This will give you the dollar amount of your automobile expense:

> 12,000 Business Miles
> × .205 Standard Mileage Rate
> $2,460 Automobile Expense (Parking fees
> and tolls may be added to this)

As of this writing, if you drive more than fifteen thousand business miles in any year, the standard mileage rate for each additional mile is eleven cents. Once you drive a vehicle sixty thousand business miles, the standard mileage rate for all mileage for that vehicle drops to eleven cents per mile. These rates are subject to change by the IRS.

Percentage of Total Operating Costs

To calculate your deductible expenses this way, keep a record of the number of miles you drive for business reasons during the year, and keep track of all of your automobile expenses. Then multiply the deductible percentage of automobile expenses times the total cost of operating your car:

$$\frac{12{,}000 \text{ Business Miles}}{20{,}000 \text{ Total Miles Driven}} = 60\%$$

> $5,000 Total Automobile Operating Costs
> × .60 Deductible Percentage
> $3,000 Automobile Expense (Parking fees
> and tolls may be added to this sum)

Since this method is based on your automobile operating costs rather than on a standard rare per mile, it's especially important to keep receipts documenting your automobile expenses.

To make sure that you are claiming the full automobile deduction the IRS allows, you should try both methods (at least in the beginning). Then, after comparing the totals, choose the method that gives you the higher deduction. In the example shown, the percentage method would give you the higher deduction. However, in a different example, the opposite may be true.

Entertainment Expenses

Business entertainment expenses also are tax deductible. To qualify as a deductible item, the entertainment expense must be ordinary and necessary in performing your consulting duties or operating your business. As with your automobile expenses, you must separate your business entertainment expenses from the nonbusiness ones. Whenever entertainment is for both business and social purposes, only the business part is deductible. For example, if you entertain a group that includes three prospective clients and one social guest, you may deduct the expenses for yourself and the three prospects, but you may *not* deduct the amount you spend on the social guest. In this instance, four-fifths of the entertainment expense is tax deductible.

In determining whether or not an entertainment expense is deductible, ask yourself if the entertainment had a clear business purpose. Was it to get new business or to encourage the continuation of an existing business relationship? If your answer is yes, then you should be able to claim the expense as a business deduction. For example, taking a prospective client to lunch or dinner is a deductible expense if you discuss business at some time during the meal.

To comply with the IRS rules on entertainment, you should keep a record of all business entertainment expenses along with the receipts or other supporting evidence to back them up. Entering a luncheon date on your desk calendar isn't enough. To be properly documented, the lunch must be backed up by the receipt for the meal.

When claiming an expense as a business entertainment deduction, you must be able to prove the following:

- The amount of the expense
- The date the entertainment took place
- The location of the entertainment, such as a restaurant or theater
- The reason for the entertainment (to promote your consulting services, to discuss a consulting project)
- The name and title (or occupation) of each person you entertained

The more specific you can be, the better, since this will add to the validity of your deductions.

Reimbursable Client Expenses

You should keep separate records of the client-related expenses for which you will be reimbursed by the client. For example, the travel expense reimbursement form on page 168 provides a record of travel expenses incurred on the client's behalf. These expenses should be billed directly to the client's account in addition to your consulting fees. Since the client is reimbursing you for the expenses, you may not deduct them from your taxes. However, the client may be entitled to do so.

YOUR TAXES

Much as you might like to ignore them, taxes are an inevitable part of doing business. If you keep good records, taxes shouldn't pose a problem for you. The nature of your consulting practice, its legal form, and its location will determine the taxes you must pay.

Federal Taxes

The two best-known federal taxes that entrepreneurs are required to pay are income tax and self-employment tax. If

**Ferris and Associates
Marketing Research**

TRAVEL EXPENSE REIMBURSEMENT FORM

Client's Name _____ Consulting Project _____

Address _____

Date				
EXPENSE Place				
Airfare				
Car Rental				
Tolls				
Gasoline				
Taxi				
Breakfast				
Lunch				
Dinner				
Hotel				
Telephone				
Tips				
Misc.				

Submitted by _____   Approved by _____

Date   _____   Date   _____

you employ other people in your consulting practice, you may also be subject to employment taxes.

Income Tax

Every business is required by law to file an annual income tax return. The form you use depends on whether your consulting firm is a sole proprietorship, a partnership, or a corporation.

If you are a sole proprietorship, you should report your business income and deductions on Schedule C (Form 1040). Attach this schedule to your individual tax return Form 1040 and submit them together. If you own more than one business, you must file a separate Schedule C for each one.

If you are a partner in a consulting firm, your income and deductions from the partnership should be reported on Schedule K-1 (Form 1065) and filed along with your individual tax return. Each of your partners should do the same, accounting for his or her income and deductions in this way. In addition, the total income and deductions for the partnership itself must be reported on Form 1065.

A corporation reports its taxable income on Form 1120. S corporations use Form 1120S. Any income or dividends that you receive from the corporation should be entered on your individual tax return. However, if you are a shareholder in an S corporation, your income and deductions should be reported in the same way that they would be in a partnership. In this instance, though, you use Schedule K-1 (Form 1120S).

Self-Employment Tax

Self-employment tax is a Social Security tax for people who are self-employed. It's similar to the Social Security tax paid by wage earners, but you pay it yourself instead of having it withheld from your paycheck. To find out more about this tax, check IRS publication 533, "Self-Employment Tax."

Estimated Tax

The IRS requires that you pay your income and self-employment taxes each year on a pay-as-you-go basis. Rather than paying them in one lump sum at the end of the tax period, you must pay them in installments by these dates:

* April 15
* June 15
* September 15
* January 15 (of the following year)

Using this method, you pay one-quarter of your total tax liability on each date until the liability is paid in full. If you discover in, say, August that you are paying too much or too little tax, you can decrease or increase the size of the remaining payments accordingly. Remember, though, that you are required to prepay at least 80 percent of your tax liability each year. If you prepay less, you may be subject to a penalty.

Try to make your estimates as accurate as possible to spare yourself that expense. When in doubt, you will do better to pay more than the amount you've estimated so as to ensure meeting the 80-percent prepayment minimum. The form you use to estimate your tax is Form 1040-ES, which can be obtained from the IRS.

Employment Taxes

If you have employees in your consulting practice, you will probably need to pay employment taxes. These taxes include:

1. Federal income tax, which you withhold from your employees' wages.
2. Social Security tax, part of which you withhold from your employees' wages and the rest of which you contribute as an employer.
3. Federal unemployment tax, which you as an employer must pay.

Report both the income tax and the Social Security tax on

Form 941, and pay both taxes when you submit the forms. Report and pay the federal unemployment tax separately, using Form 940. For more information about employment tax and which ones, if any, you must pay, read IRS publication 15, "Circular E."

State and Local Taxes

The types and amounts of state and local taxes that you as a business owner must pay will depend on where your consulting firm is located. For instance, businesses in New York and California are subject to higher rates of taxation than those in Pennsylvania and Texas. Some states have income and sales taxes; others don't. All states have unemployment taxes.

Just as the states vary when it comes to taxation, so do counties, cities, and towns within the states. Some of the taxes imposed at this level include business taxes, licensing fees, and income taxes.

To make sure that your consulting firm is meeting its state and local tax obligations, contact the authorities for your locality to determine those taxes for which you are responsible.

For more information on business taxation, refer to the IRS publications described in Chapter 9.

Index